A Gentleman's Cry

For supporting my very first book!

Women like acknowledgement and loving affection. They want a person with whom they can relate. They want a person they can trust. They want to be able to discuss problems they might be having, without difficulties. Women are mysterious, but they will show you what it feels like to be truly loved, as long as you're willing and able to accept the responsibility of a true loving relationship. You have to show them and mean it, no matter how hard it may be for you at the time. Women like men who are compassionate and understanding and someone who always genuinely cares. A woman wants a man to tell her often how important she is to him and show her that in his actions.

A Gentleman's Cry

Life of Betrayal and Dishonest Behavior

DERRICK TAYLOR

DTAYLOR Books™
ATLANTA, GA

Published by *DTAYLOR Books*™

ISBN 13: 978-0-615-36081-2
LCCN: 2010903737

First *DTAYLOR Books*™ printing, March 2010

SPECIAL THANKS:

Rachel Bohan-Editor

Natasha Buchanan-Consultant

Stan Ferrell-Inline Graphics

Latoya C.G. Wiley-Consultant

Herbert Andrews Williams Jr.-Photographer

*Acknowledgments*

To every woman who has been a part of my life
and felt that I've done her wrong, I apologize.

To my first-born son, in hopes that he
becomes a better man than his dad.

In loving memory of my grandmother, Mrs.
Arnelia Taylor, who I miss and love so much.

Most importantly, I thank God and my savior Jesus
Christ for giving me the ability to share my life.

"Everybody keeps telling me to stop saving you, because you keep living above your means. You continue to do the same old shit and not trying to change. You constantly lie about unnecessary shit. It's going to take something drastic to happen before you realize you're not fooling anybody but yourself. I don't want anything from you. All I ever did was try to help you. I'm so disgusted with you and your mentality that I don't want to call or even talk to you. You think life is a damn joke, man. There are so many people you've lied to that no one likes dealing with you. As God be my witness, I will help you this time, but you will drown from this point forward. It's your life, so do as you damn well please."

Table of Contents

Foreword

"The True Gentleman is the man whose conduct proceeds from good will and an acute sense of propriety, and whose self-control is equal to all emergencies; who does not make the poor man conscious of his poverty, the obscure man of his obscurity, or any man of his inferiority or deformity; who is himself humbled if necessity compels him humble another; who does not flatter wealth, cringe before power, or boast of his own possessions or achievements; who speaks with frankness but always with sincerity and sympathy; whose deed follows his word; who thinks of the rights and feelings of others, rather than his own; and who appears well in any company, a man with whom honor is sacred and virtue safe."

~John Walter Wayland

Introduction

When you think of a gentleman, you think of someone who has respect; someone who is responsible and caring. These are qualities I've lacked throughout my life. When I was a kid, I never imagined I would be in the predicament I'm in today. What am I talking about? I'm talking about my behavior toward the many women who have been part of my life.

I was never taught how to respect women. If a child lacks proper structure and guidance and doesn't see in their family life how to treat and respect the opposite sex, they grow up with a distorted view of relationships in general—they are raised not knowing how to return love. Growing up, I lacked this guidance. You have to start at an early age to mold a child into a loving and considerate person.

I learned to objectify women at an early age. I was taught subtly that when dealing with women, I had to be in control. I was immature, ruled by sexual intent, and extremely self-centered. I would hate on and emotionally beat down the women in my life. I seemed to destroy the women who had my back while I was involved with them.

I've asked myself many times how a woman can ever obtain respect, love, and adoration if there are people like me who act like men, but in reality are not men at all. I would go out of my way to tear down and destroy women, both physically and verbally, with slanderous lies. I would put up a front of sensitivity and caring, drawing women in only for them to later discover the real me. A real man would not viciously tear down the women who care for him. That's what a weak, spineless, gutless man does, not a real man.

So a lot has to be done on my part for me to become a good man. And if I don't change my ways, I will lose any chance I may have had to become a great man. I've been thinking about my life up to this point and about how my upbringing shaped my disrespectful behavior toward women. I have also been thinking about the relationships that I've had. I ask myself why it's so difficult for me to build a long-term, loving, and respectful relationship with a woman. What is happening that makes it so hard for me to earn a woman's trust? I once heard that love doesn't fail, but we as individuals fail—is this what happened with me?

A Gentleman's Cry

Disrespect with Intent

Chapter 1

Disrespect with Intent

I'm writing about my experiences and behavior toward women in hopes that any man who has been through what I've been through might read this and, seeing that I can speak on it and become a better person, realize that they can do the same.

I'm disappointed with the way I've treated people, especially women. I've preyed on women that I knew I could get over on. I've disrespected women verbally, and sometimes physically. Is it because of my controlling ways, or is it because I'm just a spoiled ass who always wants things to be his way? And throughout the years, I have not made any progress toward real change.

I knew this wasn't the way my mom wanted me to act towards women, but I inherited bad habits—and it wasn't that I couldn't change my ways, it was just that I didn't think these women deserved my respect. I couldn't care less about what anybody thought of me when it came to how I dealt with women. As a young adult there were only so many things that a woman could do for me:

1. Have sex with me.

2. Provide material things for me.

3. Leave me the hell alone when I felt I was finished with them.

It wasn't their fault that I treated them so carelessly. I did it because I never respected myself, much less them. I was caught up in a life of dishonesty and betrayal. I can't recall ever telling a woman the truth. Why?

1. I told myself that they all deserved the lies I was telling them. I knew women lied, too, and my objective was to beat them to it.

2. And why should they get my respect? Of course, I never took the time to actually get to know these women, because I didn't invest in anyone for too long.

I never really had a steady relationship. Since my early twenties I've had different women in and out of my life. When I noticed them beginning to develop feelings for me, I would end the relationship and begin a new journey with someone else. I refused to get caught up with one woman. If I found myself spending too much time with the same girl I would quickly distance myself. To be honest, I can count on one hand how many women I've actually cared for in my life: three. Why wasn't I able to work it out with at least one of these women? The answer is quite simple:

1. I was immature and still wanted to play games.

2. I would sabotage the situation before it progressed.

3. I only cared about the sex and the women could only be useful when they did things that would benefit me.

4. If another woman came along and did what the previous woman was doing I would start working on the new girl and get rid of the old one.

5. I constantly lied about everything.

The fact of the matter is that somebody was going to be made a fool and it wasn't going to be me. I had this attitude that I was too smooth and too much of a big-time player to get caught up with just one woman.

When it came to physical attraction, sex was the only thing on my mind. I've had sex with many women in my life, and sometimes it makes me ashamed when I reflect back on those experiences. When I was young I had the mindset, "The more women I can sleep with, the better."

*****

True Scenario: I remember my friends and I playing silly games with women, one of our favorites being to see how many pairs of panties we could collect from the women we'd slept with. We would have sex with as many girls as we could and afterward, we would collect their panties. I can remember having sex with as many as ten different women in one month, collecting their garments as if I ran a lingerie store.

*****

Every woman who was a part of my life thought they shared a bond with me; they did, but not in a relationship way. I was clearly only in it for sex and money. If a woman wanted to spend time with me it had to be on my terms. It had to be a day I chose and at the time I awarded them. I only cared about the value of my time and didn't respect how valuable their time was. In any situation it was my way or the highway. Sometimes I would make it clear what a woman was there for when they came to see me. About ninety percent of the time I spent with women was during what we called "booty-call hours." I would be out all day with my friends and when I felt the urge to be with a woman, I would then give them that late-night call. If they did come over and didn't do what I wanted them to do, I would kick them out. It didn't matter what time it was. I would then phone the next girl with whom I had a better chance to get the sex that I wanted.

The women I considered average-looking—those with a nice body and an unattractive face—had the worst of the deal. I never really gave them room for error; it was one and done. I would never be seen in public with an average-looking woman.

But behind closed doors, it was whatever I thought was necessary. I knew it was wrong to mess with these women, but I just didn't care. It was bad enough that they couldn't get a decent man; I was making it even harder for them to trust any man. I felt a woman was always beneath me and I was never going to respect them. I'm not a person who likes to get involved with someone past a certain point. I may look good on the outside but inside is a feeling I can't bear to contain, and this is why I have become the person I am today.

A Gentleman's Cry

A Woman's Worth

Chapter 2

A Woman's Worth

My approach to women was very disrespectful. The only thing that mattered to me was sex and the material things that came with it. I really had what we men think of as a "talk game," coupled with a decent look and a charming personality that made women interested in getting to know me.

1. I had a way of making women feel comfortable with me.
2. I made them feel as if they could trust me.
3. They found me funny and extremely entertaining.

They would have such a great time with me and start to think, "Hey, this guy isn't so bad." As the saying goes, "Everything is peaches and cream at the beginning of a friendship."

It wasn't long after I would meet a young lady that we would have sex. My favorite line was how I would tell women that I haven't been sexually involved for months and that I was trying to wait until either I found the right girl or until I was married (of course I wasn't looking for either of those things). My goal was to make her feel that I was a special person and that I really cared about her. But I wasn't looking for the right girl—I was looking for the right-now girl.

She would begin to feel that she was into me and within a week's time we would be sleeping together. It didn't matter whether or not it was good for her; I was just pleased to have accomplished the goals I had set for myself.

For the most part, I always knew that I was never going to see this girl again.

I began to create this list where I would write down all the names of the women I was involved with, just to keep track of how many I was sleeping with. My approach was the same every time I wanted to attract a woman—if it's not broken, don't fix it, right? It became so easy for me. My behavior was out of hand and there was no turning back.

Women say all the time that they can't find a good man.

And when they found me they certainly weren't getting a good man. I had never really been in a relationship that meant anything to me. To the women it meant a lot, but for me it was about sex, and only sex. The sole purpose of any relationship I had was to fulfill my needs and my desires. My relationships never had anything to do with the other person. I was very unpredictable and had this mystery about me that women couldn't figure out. I always played a lot and loved to say things that I really meant, but would back it up by saying it was a joke, leaving them without a clue about what to believe.

I became very good at manipulating women. I would verbally abuse them because I didn't care about their feelings, and our conversations would always turn out to revolve around me. I was never a good listener, but my attention span was even shorter when it came to listening to a woman. I didn't care about how they felt, what they were thinking, or how their day was. To me that was a waste of time. My two concerns were:

What did you buy me and when can we have sex?

I had become this out-of-control sex addict. Sex became the first and only thing on my mind when I was around a woman, and that was the only time I really wanted to be around a woman. Some women accepted this because they lacked self-esteem; some women didn't—and I wanted nothing to do with the ones who didn't accept it. They were a waste of my time.

When it came down to committing to a woman I was very picky. If she didn't have that exotic superficial look about her, I was not interested. The type of woman I was looking for had a light complexion and long, pretty hair, and was very petite—a model-type woman like those seen in music videos and movies. In bed, she had to have a freaky side because I was something of a freak myself. My family used to always tell me that I was color-struck—they weren't wrong. If she wasn't lighter than me I just wasn't that interested, especially in a relationship kind of way. I was never the romantic type. Holding hands with a woman in public was not an option. I was very disrespectful in public when I was with a woman.

I had wandering eyes that checked out every woman I saw. I didn't try to hide it; I was very rude, indeed.

Let's say that I did have a woman I was dating. There was a saying that when the summer season came, men would break up with their girlfriends just to catch the next fling that was out there. I was that guy. I hardly ever kept something serious with a woman around summertime.

I would never commit around that season because I'd always feel like I was missing out on something.

I always thought the grass was greener on the other side. My problem was that I never took the time to find out whether or not any of these women I met were a great fit for me. I never took the time to get to know them for who they were. A woman's feelings didn't matter to me—I was too far gone worrying about what I was getting out of the deal.

Why was I treating women this rudely? After awhile, I started feeling bad about my behavior. What I was really doing was putting the exclamation mark on the stereotype that women already held, that all men are dogs. Growing up with my mom and only having one sister, you would think I'd have more respect for women. I should have learned to be a respectful man toward women from seeing how men treated both my mother and sister. But I didn't—I was even worse than those men. I had no knowledge of how to treat women; lying to them was what I knew best. I could be talking to a woman and know immediately, before we had even had a conversation, that I was going to lie. Why?

1. It was easy, and I could lie myself into anything.
2. If I was really interested, I lied because I feared she wouldn't be interested in the truth.

I had a problem with blaming all women I was involved with for any wrongdoing in our relationship. There was no compromising. It was basically, "I said what I meant and that's what is going to happen." I wasn't a very understanding person.

A man pursues a woman in hopes that they bond and one day get to the point of having a family together. I was never thinking about a family, or what it took to have a family (I didn't grow up that way). Sometimes I would even intrude on other people's relationships. If I saw any signs that the woman was interested, that was my opportunity to take advantage of the situation. That became a challenge for me, to take other men's women. Knowing it was wrong didn't bother me. I had to have what I wanted. Married women were no exception. I felt I was helping them out—you know, satisfying their needs. I had my fair share of trysts with married women. I didn't care if she was committing adultery; that wasn't my problem.

Breaking up a happy home wasn't my problem, either.

I never thought about karma, or how I would feel if I had a wife who was cheating on me. Because I wasn't in that situation, it was no concern of mine. My objective was to take a woman from her man. If I began to doubt myself, then I had to accomplish that goal, just to prove to myself that I still had that game. The majority of the time I was successful, and sometimes I wasn't. And when I wasn't, I wouldn't give up.

I would hardly ever take a woman on a date, especially if I was only pretending to like them or wasn't interested in them. If we did go out, most of the time they would pay, I would only pay for something when I knew I would get something in return. I never really liked to be with a woman in public. I didn't want to take the chance of running into another woman with whom I was also involved. I hardly ever called a woman during respectable hours. If you didn't mean anything to me, you didn't have the luxury of getting that kind of respect from me.

My sexual appetite was very high. I could easily be sexually involved with three women in a single day. My goal was to meet woman and sleep with them as quickly as possible. I've enjoyed many one-night stands (If a woman wasn't talking the kind of talk I wanted to hear, she was of no interest to me for any longer than a night). It didn't help that I was living in a city that was known for having a lot of beautiful single women, and where women outnumbered men. I would have women all over town.

It was funny to me how many numbers I had in my phone and how many choices I had to make when it came down to me calling a certain type of women. I had labels for the women in my life:

1. Miss Breadwinner: the woman who would give me material things
2. Head: the woman who only gave me oral satisfaction
3. In-House: the woman I could call on for sex anytime, no matter what the situation was

And those are just a few examples. Material things were more important to me than sex. Because I could get sex on the regular, my objective was to try to get ahead financially. Tearing down a woman's self-esteem was so easy for me to do. I wasn't considering the fact that the things I was doing would come back on me, nor the fact that I may have scared these women into not trusting the next man who might come along and want more for her that I did. I was not very thoughtful when it came to that. I started thinking about my worth as a man.

1. What was my gift to women?

2. How could I be a great man and find that special woman?

I had no clue. I didn't even think I deserved to be with a woman. I was a user of women.

When I got tired of one I would easily move to the next. I believe that was my gift, to ruin every woman that I met. I was pretending to be this Prince Charming only to turn out to be a villain to women. They say physically abusing a woman is the worst thing you can do to lower their self-esteem. That may be true for the most part, but for me it verbally and mentally abusing them seemed to be far more effective.

We all know that a woman is put on this earth to make men better. I took that statement literally, because if she wasn't helping me to better myself, I had no use for her. I didn't care about her feelings or her well-being. I had the attitude that I could get any woman I wanted, and I didn't care how I went about doing it. If that was my goal, then that was the goal I would meet.

I thought women were as scandalous as men, and if that was the case I wasn't going to be played by any of them. My ultimate goals were to play women and be very sneaky about it before they got the chance to do it to me. It never occurred to me that not all women were the same.

1. Most women want to be loved.

2. Most women want that honest, strong, and reliable man for security.

My attitude didn't allow me to think that way. The fact was that I didn't trust them and used them for everything they had (my friends who were in relationships used to tell me that I may end up alone if I didn't change my approach toward women). I wanted to play the game to the fullest.

A Gentleman's Cry

Not Family-Oriented

Chapter 3

Not Family-Oriented

Many families endure pain, suffering, and plenty of ups and downs. My life may not be different from many others, but my familial background played a significant role in shaping who I am today. I share with you the trials and tribulations I encountered in my family life. I truly do not believe that a person should remain the same type of person later in life that they were growing up, despite whatever hardship they come from. Anyone and everyone can change.

I really believe that I became such a disrespectful person because of the lack of family structure I dealt with as a child. I also do believe people can change despite whatever environment they may come from. But I never really took up the personal responsibility to better myself. I never took the time to realize that how I grew up didn't have to make me who I am today, unless I let it play a role in my life.

I was born in 1975 to a 23-year-old single mother who already had three kids. Two years after I was born she had another child, my younger brother Tony. Would this be the kind of lifestyle I would grow up with as a child, trying to understand the reality of my siblings and me having different fathers? What kind of example could that set for me? As a young boy, none of that mattered because we still enjoyed each other as kids, and we were still were very close despite coming from different fathers.

As a child, I had several problems that would play a big role in my life. I had heart failure as an infant (doctors told my mother that her child was not going to survive), and I was in and out of the hospital on a weekly basis because of those severe heart complications. I was always told that I was a very hyper baby and that my heart wasn't strong enough to endure that hyperactivity. I was often unable to do the things my siblings could do. I couldn't be active the way they were. At times my mother would have to hold me in her arms just so I couldn't run and play like the other kids. I had what they called a heart murmur and had to have a tube inserted into my chest to monitor the strength of my heart.

I guess that played a big role in how I acted as an adult. I became very spoiled because of the treatment I was receiving from my mother and the rest of the family. I received different punishment than my siblings. I could essentially get anything I wanted if I just said that my heart was bothering me. Not only was that wrong of me, but it was crippling me as I grew into a man.

By the time I was five, things really hadn't gotten any better for my family and me. First of all, my mom was a single mother with no education because she had dropped out of school to support her kids. She was working dead-end jobs making very little money—certainly not enough to support the family—but doing the best that she could. I remember getting up to be dropped off to my grandmother's house every morning while my mom went to different jobs. Although we did have a place to stay, most of our time was spent with our grandmother.

*****

True Scenario: Imagine sharing a rundown, one-bedroom apartment with three other siblings and a single mother still in her early twenties, and trying to live comfortably. It wasn't great. We sometimes didn't have all the necessary things a family needed to survive. We witnessed our water, lights, and heat being cut off due to not having the money to pay the bills. And of course our mother was still young and trying to enjoy the dating life, hoping to find a man to complete her. I can still remember the different men moving in and out of my mom's life when I was kid. I didn't really know the reason, being that I was so young, but I knew it was affecting me. How?

Witnessing my mom with those different men led me to lose respect for her, so how could I respect the women I would later deal with?

*****

I guess you can compare my mom to a young mother in the twenty-first century—one who is in her teens when she has a baby out of wedlock, and looks to her mother to take care of the child because she is naïve and unprepared to do it on her own because of her inability to make good decisions. I'm by no means judging my mom, but as a kid witnessing those things, you get a confusing example and become angry that things are going so badly for your family, and the majority of the time you end up blaming the head of your household.

Because of my mother's situation, we would sometimes go to live with my grandmother for a while. It became a comfortable setting for us. After staying with our grandmother for such a long period of time we would start calling her "mama" and referring to our biological mom by her first name. We knew she was our mom, but we didn't call her that.

We were just not oriented as a family. The conditions I grew up in may not have been that different from other families—there are ups and downs in all phases of life—but it seemed that all we encountered were the down times. To me, everything my family tried to accomplish faded from existence. After many years of living with my grandmother, I recall my mother working temporary jobs to provide for us. It became so hard for my mother to enjoy her life because she'd had kids at such a young age and she never had the time to enjoy the luxury of living the lifestyle any woman in her twenties would want to live.

Sometimes we weren't her top priority. The money she did make would ultimately be spent on herself, as she was trying to hang out with her friends, drinking and smoking. Just as many single parents do, she always relied on her mother (my grandmother) to raise her kids—I'm not saying that she didn't love us, but we just weren't her main focus in life.

My mom never had any real help from our fathers. The little help she did get did not go to us. We hardly ever lived a stable life under our mother's vision. We constantly moved around, and at times my mom couldn't even make payments on our living arrangements. Sometimes we would live with different relatives, separating us for long periods of time. I might live with one aunt on one side of town while my brothers would live with some other family member on the other side of town. We were very distant when it came time to stay with some of our other relatives. We didn't get along with most of them because of the reputation my mother had with them. They thought of my mother as irresponsible and someone who only called on them when she needed their help. My mom would sometimes tell them that she would pay them to keep us and when it was time for them to collect the money she wouldn't follow through on her promise.

1. I guess that's a flaw I inherited from my mother
2. I guess I'm more like my mom, because I had a hard time getting along with the people around me.

The only good thing about moving around so much was that we were able to witness a lot and make plenty of new friends—aside from that it was a nightmare. We never had the luxury of having decent clothes or nice shoes. Because of our misfortunes, my brothers and I would often borrow clothes from our neighbors because they knew we didn't have much. Due to our poor living arrangements, my mom had to apply for welfare. But it didn't help much because we would hardly ever see anything from the welfare money. Sometimes I even saw my mom selling her food stamps for money just so she could enjoy her life and hanging out with her friends.

My mom had a problem with drinking and smoking. The money she did make was pretty much spent on alcohol and drugs. Her alcohol of choice was gin and her drug of choice was marijuana. I would sometimes witness my mom rolling a joint as if it was a cigarette and she would sometimes even smoke it around us. As a kid, I really didn't know a lot, but what I did know was that our living situation wasn't great and we just had to learn to adjust. We had to make the best of what we had. We didn't have the answers all the time, but one thing my brothers and I did have was street smarts.

In order for us to get what we wanted, we had to work at a young age. I remember my uncles and aunts giving us money to go play their daily numbers, and I would make at least fifty cents a day doing that. Just as they have the lottery today, we had local gambling in our neighborhood. It was illegal, but we didn't know too much about that. No one was going to give us anything, so the only thing we knew how to do at such a young age was hustle. If we didn't try to make it on our own, we knew that we wouldn't get much help from anyone else.

After living in many different places and after upgrading from a small one-bedroom, we were finally able to afford another apartment. This time the apartment had two bedrooms, but there was still not that much space. My brothers and I still had to share one bedroom. It wasn't very comfortable, not to mention that my younger brother was a bed-wetter. Not only were we dealing with that issue, but because this apartment wasn't very clean, we also had a problem with pests and rodents. But we had to make the best of what we were able to afford because my mom didn't have a decent job and we were living on welfare, which didn't give us much.

Our biggest problem was food. That was always an issue with us. We had to know how to manage the food we did have, and be considerate enough to remember that we had to eat the next day. I can still remember waking up and seeing roaches all around the kitchen when we would go to get something to eat. When that was the case, we just hoped and prayed that we didn't get sick.

We were called "the poor family" by some of the people in our neighborhood. Other families would know that if we came to their homes we were there for one reason and one reason only, and that was to try and get something to eat from them. Sometimes they would welcome us and sometimes they wouldn't.

We never saw our fathers in our life. My mom had many different men come in and out of our lives—I guess she was trying to find a man who would help her. But I didn't often see the same man more than a few times, and I saw her bring home all types of men.

I guess they were there for the pleasure of being with my mom.

Sometimes I would hear my mom arguing with those men. If that ever was the case we immediately became very protective of our mother.

1. We didn't allow any man to put his hands on our mother.

2. If a man was really there to help our mother then of course we were all for it, but anything else would have been uncivilized.

After a long period of time, seeing my mom with these men and none of them really staying in her life, I began to realize:

What man wanted a woman who had five kids?

At that, a woman on welfare who lacked an education or a good job to support her kids.

It was useless. We started to accept the fact that my mom would never have the family that she may have wanted. We would constantly hear that we were to blame for her inability to keep a man in her life. Her finger would always be pointed at us.

1. She would say that if she didn't have us, maybe her life would be easier.

2. She would sometimes say that she wished we were never even born.

None of us asked to come into this world, but she did have her way of showing us that it was our fault for being here and making her life hell. We were never really close as a family and after learning that we were to blame for her misfortune, we became even more divided.

Very little changed for my family. After several months in our apartment, we began to encounter even more problems. There were times when it would rain and floodwaters would run into our apartment. After experiencing several floods, we adapted to the idea that when it rained we would have to deal with the fact that it would flood our apartment. Other situations we faced were:

1. Having our lights and water turned off because my mom was unable to pay the bills.
2. Sometimes being unable to make our rent payments.

We became the joke of our entire neighborhood. And yet, dealing with all those circumstances, we still managed to stay positive.

*****

True Scenario: One afternoon a huge storm passed through our city. It rained all day and into the night. As the rain got heavier and heavier the water began to seep into our apartment, rising higher and higher. We soon realized that everything in the apartment was going to be destroyed, not to mention that the five young boys in the apartment didn't know how to swim. The worst thing about our apartment was its location. It was near a wooded area and sometimes we would see snakes. All of this came into consideration when our house flooded. Luckily, some friends in the neighborhood—remembering my mother with five little boys—came to our rescue. One by one, we jumped on their backs and they carried us through the waters to safety.

Due to this misfortune, our family was again separated, with each of us sent to different family members and trying to figure out what our next move would be. When that flood hit, we lost the few possessions we had. What little clothes and shoes we had were gone. All we had were the clothes on our backs, and those clothes were wet and smelled bad. Our neighbors donated clothes that they couldn't wear. It was a disaster. We faced one setback after another, but we had to keep our composure.

*****

I remember jumping for joy when my mom was finally able to get her first home. We were able to have more space to move around and enjoy living life the way that it should be. Although we didn't have much furniture at the time, we did the best that we could. The house needed a lot of work; I could still tell that we were not as fortunate as the other kids because of all the homes in our neighborhood, ours was the worst-looking one. But at least we had a home—well, at least for a little while we did.

One night something drastic happened. I awoke to my mom screaming for us to get up and get out of the house. I got up and saw smoke everywhere—our brand new house had caught on fire. Once again, our lives were at a turning point. Everything had burned in the fire and our house was gone. How much can one family go through in such a short period of time? I thought that we were the only family having a hard time and I decided that I just didn't care anymore. That was the attitude I adopted as I got older. I lost trust in everything and blamed my family's misfortune on anything and anyone. And that vengeful spirit stayed with me as I matured.

I was sick and tired of the problems we were constantly facing. I didn't want to move anymore, I just wanted to be stable and have a solid, reliable home. I could sense my mom throwing in the towel as she began to cry much more often. She had nowhere else to turn and she couldn't get the help from her family that she needed. She would sometimes leave for days on end, trying to find a solution. We didn't understand it at the time but we knew she wasn't herself anymore. We started to think that we were in the way of her achieving the better life she so desperately wanted. We were a failure as a family. The bad decisions my mom made as a kid kept us from having the life that most young children dream of having. We never spent holidays together as a family; we never enjoyed Christmas and Thanksgiving as a family. When our birthdays came around, we didn't have birthday parties. Our goal was to just try and make it the best way we knew how.

A Gentleman's Cry

Adolescent Bad Behavior

Chapter 4

Adolescent Bad Behavior

Kids are a product of their environment. But despite any obstacles your child might face, always try to be in their life and raise them to be a good person. Times do get tough, but never give up on your child. Always believe that they can make a difference.

As we grew up, my siblings and I tried to become closer as a family and started hanging out with one another more often. My grandmother's house was convenient to the other kids in the neighborhood, so we embraced it. We started meeting other kids—some were fun to be around, and others were not so great—but because of what we had been through, we were accustomed to the bad and tough behavior of other kids.

It didn't get any better once we started to develop and hang out with the kids in the neighborhood. We were all different ages and I saw my siblings starting to hang out with their respective age groups, a development I disapproved of because I wanted us to remain close to each other. I didn't understand that we could go in different directions, but still remain close as a family. I was afraid to hang out with the other kids in the neighborhood because I was shy and spoiled and wanted things to be my way, and I had never learned how to make friends without my brothers around me. I started hanging out by myself and became very antisocial.

I started acting out toward my brothers and wanted to be by myself all the time. I was only six years old.

Everyone noticed the change in my behavior and didn't approve of it. I became this hyper kid with so much energy, and no one had any idea what was wrong with me. I became so energetic and poorly behaved to the point that no one wanted to have anything to do with me. Why?

1. I was a terrible kid who enjoyed seeing another person injured or in pain.
2. I would go places I knew I had no business going, just so that people would worry about me—I was screaming for attention.
3. I knew I would get away with my behavior because I had an excuse—my heart condition. If I was punished for anything, all I had to do was say that my heart was bothering me.

When I knew I was going to get a whipping, I would immediately yell, "My heart hurts!" My siblings would see that and get mad at me, then distance themselves from me. Noticing that, I became even more disobedient to everyone.

No one knew me better than my oldest brother, Michael. Although he wouldn't let me hang with him, he did his best to challenge me to become a better person. Unfortunately, challenging me didn't change my behavior—it only made it worse. Anything Michael told me would go in one ear and out the other, rendering it useless. I couldn't be helped; at least not by my family—we weren't the type of family who would sit down together and talk through our problems. They were always solved outside of the home.

Our problems grew worse when we went out in our neighborhood. Everything we learned, we learned hanging out in the streets. The more we got to know our neighborhood, the more trouble we got into. We never had allowances given to us. The only thing we knew how to do well was stealing.

*****

True Scenario: I remember going to grocery stores with my brothers almost daily to steal candy. Sometimes we did it for fun, but most of the time we did it because we had to find a way to eat. We became so accustomed to stealing that we knew if we stole and got away with it that we would be fine that day.

I remember I wore this big green jacket with fur around the hood, as if it was zero-below outside, but it was actually summertime. I would walk into the store and proceed to the candy aisle, grabbing a handful of family-sized packs of Snickers bars and Butterfingers. After I loaded up my jacket I would leave the store as if no one saw me. It had become a normal thing for me and my brothers. Was stealing helping my character? No, but what I wanted, I would do everything in my power to get.

*****

I remember my first day of school; I was entering the first grade, and this was another new challenge for me. Right away I decided that I had to become the center of attention at school. I started being angry with teachers and students for no reason. I picked on girls because I knew I could dominate them. I had to make numerous trips to the principal's office. I just became a terrible child. I couldn't really make friends at the school. I had gotten this reputation as a bully and no one wanted to be around me. When my class took field trips, I could never go because I was always in trouble. However, there was one trip that I did take often during my school year.

I remember a white man in a red truck coming to get me from school and taking me to this big office building miles away from my school. I was placed in a room all by myself with lots of toys and games. I would have so much fun, but then realized that I was the only one playing in this room everyday. Why? I mean, this man was so nice that he would give me practically anything

I asked for. Whether everybody hated me or they didn't want me in school, I had no idea.

The next thing I realized was that this man was giving me pills to take on a daily basis. They were these small white pills that tasted sweet, so I started thinking they were some kind of mint or some kind of candy I was receiving as a reward. I started asking my mom questions the man I was leaving school with and what these pills he was giving me were. I finally learned:

1. The man I was leaving with everyday was a psychiatric doctor.

2. The pills I thought were candy turned out to be Ritalin, which subdued my hyperactivity and energetic, disordered behavior.

3. I was diagnosed with Attention Deficit Disorder.

My ADD was so out of control that I would do things to people that were so bad that I would not remember what happened most of the time. I was really never punished for the things I did; I was only confronted. When I arrived back at school I noticed I was being placed into classes with other kids who behaved like me. I thought to myself, "Now I finally have friends I can relate to, kids who share the same passion as me." But I started noticing things and began to pay attention to certain details. I wasn't with the kids from my neighborhood. I would see them going to lunch as I would be leaving lunch, and I started to understand that my classroom was in a trailer away from the school and I wondered what the difference was. Well, the difference was that they were in regular classes and I was in special classes with kids who needed special attention. I realized that if I was going to be reunited with my peers, I was going to have to get my act together. And how was I going to do that? I couldn't function and pay attention long enough to help myself achieve that. I ended up repeating the first grade. Later, in my adolescent years, I began to focus more and more on my schoolwork and excelling in the classroom. I was able to do this because my past and my reputation as a disrespectful child meant that I didn't really have a lot of friends, enabling me to focus more and more on my work. I remember being in a fifth-grade average class that guaranteed I would be with some of my friends from my neighborhood, and I thought that was where I needed to be. But the challenge was beneath me. I excelled far more than my friends and was given a more challenging offer: later that year I was moved to what they called an above-average class where I was united with a more predominantly white peer group. That was something new for me, considering where I was raised. My friends started to see that I had left their classroom and they started to distance themselves from me, calling me names and telling me that I thought I was better than them. After all that I became rebellious and didn't want to be where I was in school. So I started letting my grades slip just so I could fail and prove to them that I was still like them. I just wanted to be accepted by my friends and didn't realize what was best for me and for my future. My schoolwork became a distant second to my friends. No matter how hard I tried to fit in, I realized that I was not going to satisfy everybody. I had become a joke.

Once the bad guy who had earned that kind of bad-guy respect, I was now the boy who became the victim. My family had no money, which meant that I could not get clothes, shoes, or anything that a normal family would pick up from the mall. I remember my brothers and I sharing clothes over the course of the school week. My friends started to notice, and that's when the torture began. I knew I had to fend for myself, so my attitude became really selfish. I stopped caring about anything. I started picking fights and no one wanted to be around me. Although I was bad as hell, I started focusing on my class work more so that I could move on to the next grade and just hope my friends would be left behind.

Now a thirteen-year-old in the sixth grade, the school introduced sports programs that I was able to join. I remembered how gifted my brothers and I used to be with sports when we were little, and I knew I had to try to excel at sports again. My oldest brother Michael, who was three years older than me and in high school, excelled in basketball. So I started distancing myself from my friends who teased me, and I started hanging with Michael a lot more. I could see the change in him and how much people wanted to be around him—and I wanted to be my brother. But before this change in my life, there was a drastic change for my younger brother Tony.

It was the summer before my sixth-grade year and, being that my two older brothers and my sister were pretty much never around our apartment, I was left to look after Tony. I remember one afternoon I had a fever that was so high that I couldn't bear to get out of bed. I heard this loud screaming and the front door burst open, making me leap out of bed. I proceeded to close my door, thinking it was the neighborhood dogs that got loose (there were some huge dogs in our neighborhood who would run free sometimes), but it wasn't—it was the sound of my mother screaming and my younger brother shouting, " I can't see, I can't see!" Tony had been the victim of a gunshot to the eye, leaving him blind in his left eye. I can still so clearly remember seeing all that blood in the house and on his shirt. My mom was so scared that she ran out of the house to go next door to ask for help. We were trying to not call an ambulance (we couldn't afford it) and we didn't have a car of our own, so our next-door neighbor took Tony to the hospital. I was so upset that my fever was no longer a factor, and all I could think about was getting revenge on whoever did this to Tony. (That never happened because I never got a chance to find the boy who had done it.)

You would think something that drastic would bring the family together, but between Tony and me it didn't. I felt as if I had failed to protect my little brother. I started thinking I was neither dependable nor reliable, and those characteristics seemed to stick as a label throughout my adolescent and teenage years. Oddly enough, the financial gain from the accident would bring us closer because we received government benefits from Tony losing his eye. The disability checks served my mom great purpose. She was the co-signer—Tony was only ten at the time—and she had sole possession of those disability checks. She would relinquish those checks as if they were addressed to her. Although Tony and I didn't receive any of the money, not even new clothes so that we could fit in at school. We saw my mom enjoying life more and, I must say, we were eating a little better than usual.

When I was thirteen we were off and moving again. This time the country side of town was more suitable for my mother. Again I made more new friends, but this time it was a little different. These friends were more into girls, and at that point in my life I had never even kissed a girl, much less what these guys were doing to girls. It was still during the summer before sixth grade when I met Sam. He had a reputation of being good with girls—we're talking actually having sex with girls (Sam was at least two years older than me). One day we were hanging out at his house when we heard a girl he knew calling for him from next door. I guess that was some kind of hint that she was home by herself because we proceeded to head next door. As we entered her house, she was standing there naked; I was amazed and my hormones were raging. I didn't know what it was at the time, but whatever it was it was a good feeling. Sam laid down with this girl and all I could hear was the sound of two bodies colliding and the sound of the girl's voice, as if she was in pain. As her noises subsided and I could no longer hear their bodies coming together, I heard my name being called to come into the room. I went in and the girl was lying on the ground, still naked, and Sam told me that she wanted me and that I should take off my clothes. Without hesitation I did just that. He handed me a condom, which I knew nothing about, and I put it on and began having sex with this girl. I had no idea what I was doing, but I knew it felt good to do it. Then a weird thing started to happen. I started feeling funny, like I was wetting the bed, so I jumped up and looked at my friend and said, "What is that?" Sam looked at me and, laughing, said, "You had an orgasm and you're a man now." I realized I was not a virgin anymore, and I went hopping and skipping home because I had just lost my virginity at the age of thirteen. My life with girls would never be the same after that.

Coming back to reality from the summer, I still had problems getting along with other kids. I made some friends; I lost some friends. And the friends I lost became my enemies. Fight after fight, things didn't get any better. But the difference this time was that Michael became more and more a part of my life, trying to teach me right from wrong. The more he tried, the more it went through one ear and straight out the other. I remember Michael telling me the only way to fend for myself was to get involved with sports like he did. I knew I had the skills, but I didn't apply myself enough—I wasn't motivated. It wasn't until I had actually seen Michael perform in a game that I became really interested in pursuing sports. I saw how he and his friends would act around each other, like they were brothers. So I began to want that. After playing football and basketball for a while I started to gain that brotherhood. The difference was that I used that popularity to control the people around me, because I knew I was the shit. That was the beginning of another trait that would follow me into my later years. The more popular I became in sports, the more a crowd grew—a crowd of girls. My relationship with girls became so easy that I could get the attention of any girl in school I wanted—at least that was what I thought at the time. It turned out it was only because I was this great athlete that everyone wanted to be around during those respective seasons; I couldn't have felt any more used than that.

As my relationship with sports grew stronger, my dedication to my schoolwork faded. I ended up flunking the seventh grade because of my poor decisions. I never took anything seriously except for my relationship with sports. To get myself back on track I enrolled in summer school, but that turned out to be a bad investment because the only thing I did was drop out. I thought I was too good for summer school. I had also become quieter, another trait that would follow me into my later years. The school year began with me restarting the seventh grade. I was so embarrassed that I really wanted to drop out of school. I thought there was no reason for me to even be there. So I became determined and tried really hard to succeed that year. I told myself that I was not going to give up again. I had become a joke to so many people. It had gotten to the point where I was really just talking out the side of my head. No one pays attention to a failure who makes false promises. I became a distraction to the people around me who took their schoolwork seriously. I had to do something to regain the trust of my peers, but what could I do? No one had any faith in me anymore because they thought I was dumb and only cared about sports. But how could I play sports if I didn't have the grades to do it? I really applied myself and began to do what was necessary to pass the seventh grade. Damn, I was dumb. The end of the school year arrived and all my friends were going to high school, but I was headed to the eighth grade—middle school again, or so I thought. But when I received my report card, I saw that I would be permitted to skip the eighth grade and enter ninth grade with the rest of my class. I was jumping for joy. I was going to be in high school with my two older brothers, Michael and James, and my friends from middle school. What a blessing that was—or was it?

Now in high school and reunited with my friends, I became calmer, but seemed to be more arrogant person in the eyes of many of my friends. I got ahead of myself, but some of my friends still thought of me as a joke. They would say things like:

1. I didn't have an eighth-grade education.

2. I skipped a grade because I was too old and not because of my hard work.

3. I sometimes felt bad about the things they were saying, but I knew what a better situation I was in at this point. And there were marked differences between middle school and high school:

4. I was around people who were thinking about and pursuing college.

5. I was around people who actually had an idea of what they wanted to do with their lives.

Those were things that I wanted, and having Michael around to guide me would help me succeed (at least that's what I thought). I could begin to see a pattern in my behavior. This time not only were sports a big part of my life, I also had to deal with girls. It didn't help that I was the younger brother of a star basketball player—it got me the attention I was seeking. I would feed off my brother's accomplishments and use them to my advantage. Not only was that not the right thing to do, but it would cripple me in years to come.

A Gentleman's Cry

Creating An Image

Chapter 5

Creating An Image

Life can be difficult. People are always looking for an influence—someone to look up to, someone to emulate. You can set the example; be the person that people want to be like. You can help change the world by changing yourself.

*****

True Scenario: From 1992 to 1994 I excelled in basketball. I was six feet, four inches tall, about 185 pounds, and could play any guard positions on the basketball court extremely well. I was recruited by several Division I college basketball teams. I was one of the top basketball players in the state of Georgia. I was honored with All-State selection, I earned *Street & Smith*'s All-American, All-Region honors, and I was nominated to the 1994 McDonald's All-American Team.

I wanted so much to be like my brother Michael. He got the attention of so many girls in high school. I would see women fight over him and sneak around with him. Being only sixteen years old, I thought that was the coolest thing on the planet. And I wanted to be just like him. So that I could be at least half the person he was, I started stealing his clothes to wear to school to portray his image. Was it helping me that I wanted to be so much like Michael? At the time, yes, but in later years, I let myself get out of control.

*****

At the end of the year Michael was off to Auburn University on a basketball scholarship. Earlier that year, his team had won the state basketball championship. I worked extremely hard the summer after he left, thinking only of my brother's accomplishments. That year turned out to be great. After awhile, though, I lost my sense of focus and started hanging around the wrong crowds. And of course, not having my brother there didn't help at all.

1. The selfishness I had exhibited when I was a kid started to resurface.

2. I wanted attention that I thought I wasn't getting.

3. My grades were getting worse.

I was becoming a failure again. Focusing only on sports and girls instead of my grades, the worst thing that could happen to a student athlete happened to me—I was kicked off my high school basketball team. Having basketball taken away from me, I truly gave up. At the young age of seventeen, I went from bad to worse almost overnight. I started drinking, skipping school, and I even started smoking marijuana with some distant friends. The sports family that I once had would look at me differently when I would try to hang out with them. I was not a part of that brotherhood like I once was—they saw me as a total loser.

The more I started feeling bad for myself, the more I started drinking. I just didn't have the drive I once had. I was becoming nobody and the path I was on led to either jail or death. Michael heard about me not doing the things I needed to do to get back on track and tried to reach out to me. Once again, it went through one ear and out the other. Repeating my pattern from the past I flunked out again, and there was nowhere for me to turn. I didn't have the type of mother who cared whether or not I succeeded. And if she did, she didn't show it. It was like I had to either make it or be nothing at all, as long as when I did finish school, I left the house. With that kind of support I didn't care what happened to me. Jail would have been paradise for me, considering what I was going through.

*****

True Scenario: It was a Saturday night and my drinking habits had increased severely to the point where I just had to have it on a regular basis. My friends Sam and Richard and I decided to go buy some alcohol and pick up some marijuana so that we could have a good time. After we'd gotten everything we headed back to the house, drinking and smoking all night. We were drunk and high, and we decided to head to the Georgia Southern University campus in Statesboro to see some college girls we'd met. As we got to the parking lot, campus security pulled us over because we had a tail light out. We did our best to hide our weed and alcohol. My heart was pounding out of my chest and the sweat was dripping from my body. The security officer asked us to get out of the car. They noticed the smell of beer on our breath and in the car. The officer asked if we had been drinking, and as scared as I was, I answered, "Yes sir, officer, we were drinking." We all had to take a Breathalyzer test, which revealed that we were over the legal limit. We were arrested and charged with minor possession of alcohol, a sentence that carried one year of probation under our parents' supervision. We were booked, had our photos taken, released to our parents, and also suffered the embarrassment of having our names printed in the local newspaper. Talk about a major disaster to my reputation—I was seen as the guy with so much potential who had become a disappointment to his hometown.

*****

I was determined to turn myself around after that. I vowed to take advantage of any opportunity that would come my way. Nevertheless, I ended up failing the tenth grade and once again found myself in summer school. But this time things were going to be different. I passed summer school and got to where I needed to be to secure my own legacy in the high school world and became the man again. That year, 1993, things got a little better for me. My skills as a great basketball player emerged and I was named to my region's all-tournament team. Our basketball team was one of the best teams in the state.

When I turned eighteen my relationship with girls became increasingly more interesting. During my eleventh-grade year I started experimenting more and more with girls—shall I say, on a more physical level. I could treat a woman wrong and not care how they felt about it. This would be a trait that I would soon carry into adulthood. Girls became a stepping stone for me. After regaining my credibility my attitude became extremely arrogant.

You'd think that I would have learned my lesson by that point; but trust me when I say I didn't get any better.

But before all that could take place, things took another turn for the worse—the first thing being that I had to witness my younger brother get arrested on drug charges, which could have only been prevented if I was in his life. It was a devastating thing for me to see my younger brother receive prison time at the age of sixteen. Knowing there was nothing I could do, I just prayed his situation would get better.

The night after my brother was sent off, I thought it was all over for me. Then the strangest thing happened. As I was sleeping the heart failure I had as a kid struck again.

That night I jumped out of bed and proceeded to the kitchen to try and drink a glass of water, thinking that would help calm my racing heartbeat. I couldn't swallow the water and started pacing back and forth in front of my mother in the living room. My mom asked me what was wrong and the only thing I could do was point to my chest and pass out. The next thing I remember is waking up in the hospital with my heart on monitors and tubes running in and out of my body. The diagnosis was that I had a severe irregular heartbeat. My only concern was whether or not I could play basketball again and, unfortunately, the doctor didn't think it was a good idea for me to continue to play sports at the time. I was devastated. I had to go to therapy for about two months before they finally cleared me to play again. It was my senior year and I excelled on the basketball court. I received All-State honors and was nominated to the McDonald's All-American Team.

Despite my struggles I graduated from high school in 1994. Because I didn't get a qualifying score on my SAT, I ended up receiving an athletic scholarship to play basketball at LB Wallace Community College in Andalusia, Alabama. I thought I was on my way to a better life. This was the most I had ever accomplished and I thought I was going to be okay.

After receiving this scholarship, the only thing I had to do was get to college, do what it took to succeed, and graduate. But none of that happened; that part of my life became a wasted opportunity. After just one semester I quit and no longer wanted any part of that institution. I had only played a total of thirteen games for the basketball team. I was at a community college in a small town, and I thought I was better than that. I left college, moved back home to Statesboro to live with my mother, and got a job at a Shoney's restaurant, where I washed dishes and was a short-order cook.

So I was this college dropout with no experience, working in a restaurant as a cook.

The most embarrassing thing was seeing the classmates and teachers who once believed in my potential look down on me for giving up on a good education and an amazing opportunity to play college basketball, the sport I loved so much. I felt devastated working in this restaurant, trying to hide everything. But did it get any better? No, it only got worse.

*****

True Scenario: I was heading home one day after work, and as I got closer to the house I saw all of my mom's furniture sitting out in the front yard. When I got to the front porch, I saw two men continuing to take all of our furniture out of the house. It turned out my mom was being evicted. It was the most embarrassing thing that I could imagine. I can remember the school bus that came through the neighborhood, dropping the kids off, only to see them laughing at my mom and me as we gathered our things from the yard and tried to think of what to do next.

*****

Dropping out of college and seeing my mom evicted was too much for me to handle. I had to figure out how to make this situation better. I wasn't thinking of going back to college, but rather how I could make some fast money. I ended up turning to friends who I knew were doing the wrong things to make money—they were selling drugs. I was curious about how to sell drugs myself, but because I didn't know too much about that business, my friends gave me the job of a drug runner. A runner was the person who would take a large amount of drugs to a specific location, unlike a dealer standing on the corner to sell his goods.

After dealing drugs for a year I realized that I could be missing any chance I had left to correct my life, and I knew I needed to get out. But it was not until I got stopped by a police officer on my way to make a drop-off that I actually followed through with that. That moment, I knew God was with me; when the police stopped me I had drugs with me—not to mention I had been drinking and smoking with my friends earlier that day. But the only thing the police asked for was my I.D. I was scared as hell and praying my heart out. I knew right then that since God got me off the hook I would never deal with drugs again.

After giving the drug game up that year I enrolled at East Georgia College for a semester and then at Middle Georgia College for a year of studies to get myself back on track. But again, it didn't happen. Despite everything I had been through, I quit college just like I had before. I was academically suspended. I had no focus and no drive. I found myself back at home again, doing absolutely nothing. I had no responsibilities, I had no life, and all of my friends were nowhere to be found.

1. I had no goals
2. No plans
3. And no motivation.

At this point, I had no choice but to get a job and try and do something with my life. I ended up working in a warehouse loading trucks and making little to no money at all. I had bad habit of blowing the money that I did make—I was very flamboyant and always living above my means. This was a bad habit to have and one that I would carry into adulthood.

After working this job for at least a year, I convinced my sister to co-sign with me my very first car. She agreed, and I wish now that she hadn't. The car was a 1995 Chevy Cavalier. It was a blue two-door coupe. I fell so in love with that car that the only thing I forgot to do was actually make the payments on the car—what an irresponsible thing to do. After about a month or so of making no payments I got a phone call from my sister accusing me of not paying the car notes. I insisted that I had, but I was lying. (Lying became a big part of my life.) After denying the fact that I wasn't making payments on the car, it got repossessed.

Everything about me had become a lie. I would lie about the littlest things just to get ahead. It got to the point where I would lie to my mom and tell her that I still had a job when I didn't. Eventually she got fed up with my behavior and kicked me out of the house. I had nowhere to go and when I refused to leave, she did the only thing I thought she would never do—she called the police on me. I was headed for the worst. I ended up staying at different places, not knowing where I would be the next day. It got so bad for me that my friends didn't want to be around me anymore. After that I really had nowhere to turn. I remember crying and crying because I couldn't depend on anybody. I lost faith in myself and didn't care what happened to me. The one person I did believe in was Michael, and he was hundreds of miles away in Baton Rouge, Louisiana. I figured that was my only option to turn my life around, so I picked up a pay phone and called him. I begged him to come get me, and after talking for several minutes he agreed. The next day I was on my way to live with my brother in Louisiana.

A Gentleman's Cry

Shoes Too Big to Fill

Chapter 6

Shoes Too Big to Fill

> *This is an example of how so many of us are still working things out on some level, though some of us dare not admit it. Become your own person and believe in yourself, because if you don't, no one else will.*

I thought then that everything was going to be just fine. My life in Louisiana seemed to be exactly what I needed. I was beginning a new phase in my life and starting fresh. I was going to do what was necessary to become a better person. Just like when we were younger, Michael was something of a father figure to me. I always wanted to be like him and have the things he had. He always stayed on me to do the right things, and I would listen to him, but just couldn't do what he said. So the saga continued.

I was in a different state with different surroundings. That meant that the person I truly was would not be recognizable in these new surroundings.

1. I could start fresh and give the image of being a great person with a great background.
2. I wouldn't be known as a liar or a manipulator.

I had no intention of changing who I was. My brother laid down several rules, but I couldn't follow them.

1. I had to get a job
2. Help out with the bills
3. And save as much money as I could.

I didn't really do any of that. I got the job only to lose it. I didn't help out with the bills much, and I didn't save any money. I was doing the same thing I was doing back home in Statesboro, Georgia, only I was doing it in Baton Rouge, Louisiana.

I did meet and date people there, but it was only for pleasure—nothing serious. I knew once I got to Baton Rouge that I wasn't going to live here. My goal was to get whatever I wanted out of the people I met. After about eight months I met a beautiful light-skinned woman named June (I had this big thing for light-skinned women. I would date women with darker complexions, but I was more attracted to the lighter-skinned women in a relationship capacity). From the moment I met June I fell for her, but I lied to her about everything. She would ask me questions like where I was from to what college I attended, and all I could think about was impressing her. My mind was screaming at me to tell her the truth and not just what I thought she wanted to hear, but I lied anyway.

1. Where are you from? Atlanta (really Statesboro).
2. What school did you attend? Georgia Southern (really LBWCC).

Any question she asked me, I responded with lie after lie. The more we hung out, the more lies I told. I ended up losing her, but it did not stop me from pursuing other girls.

By the end of my stay in Louisiana, my ways still hadn't changed. My brother was really getting tired of my shit and decided it was time for me to be on my own. I knew he was serious this time because he had landed a job in Atlanta and had begun to pack up his apartment. I had no option but to go back home, which I knew would be a disaster. I had no money saved up and only had a month to work out a solution.

I quickly went to several job interviews, but one stood out from the rest: an interview was with Heilig Meyers Furniture for a sales associate position. I borrowed some slacks and a tie from my brother and headed to the interview. When I arrived there was a long line of applicants, mostly college students. They had resumés and references, not to mention a college education. I had none of these things, but what other choice did I have? I didn't want to go back to Statesboro. The line got shorter and shorter, and finally it was my turn to be interviewed.

I went into the office and there were two white men sitting at a table. I was so nervous I was sweating bullets. They asked me for my resumé; I didn't have one. They asked me for references; I had none. I was asked if I had any prior skills at being a sales associate and I told them that I had never done that type of work. They smiled and threw me a pen and asked me to sell it to them. Well, trust me when I tell you that I made that pen seem as if that was the only pen to have. They were shocked and impressed. They thanked me and said that they would get in touch with me if they needed me.

The only things that would have kept me from getting that job were my lack of education and experience.

I went home, saw my brother, and immediately started packing my things. I was doomed. It felt as if I had been in prison and was now leaving the premises. I had to call my mom to ask if I could come home—something I definitely didn't want to do. When I got to the phone to make that call, I noticed the message light blinking on the phone and Michael told me to check it. The message was for me. It was the furniture company calling to tell me that I got the job. What a relief that was.

After a month of working there it was time to move to Atlanta with my brother, and I had to find a way to transfer my job. It was 1999 and I had only been in Louisiana for a year. My brother was already packed and ready to go. I had only been with the company for a month, so in order for me to make this happen I had to come up with a convincing story. I did what I do best: I lied.

I told them that my stepfather had colon cancer and I needed to go back home to help take care of him.

I really knew right then I could lie about anything as long as it benefited me. That lie was so convincing that the transfer was made and I was off to Atlanta, Georgia.

A Gentleman's Cry

Living Life Without A Purpose

Chapter 7

Living Life Without A Purpose

What is the meaning of life? How can purpose, fulfillment, and satisfaction be found? How can something of lasting significance be achieved? So many people have never stopped to consider these important questions. They look back years later and wonder why their relationships have fallen apart and why they feel so empty, even though they may have achieved what they set out to accomplish. An athlete who had reached the pinnacle of his career was once asked what he wished someone would have told him when he first started playing. He replied, "I wish that someone would have told me that when you reach the top, there's nothing there." Many goals reveal their emptiness only after years have been wasted in their pursuit.

People pursue many things, thinking that in them they will find meaning. Some of these pursuits include business success, wealth, good relationships, sex, entertainment, and doing good deeds. People have testified that while they achieved their goals of wealth, relationships, and pleasure, they were still left with a deep void inside; a feeling of emptiness that nothing seemed to fill.

My responsibilities began to take a backseat when it came to my social life. I was in Atlanta, a city much larger than Baton

Rouge, with a lot more to do. Instead of challenging myself in this new environment and trying to grow up, I just got myself into more trouble. Why?

1. I had a job (so I had money I could blow).
2. I had just been approved for my very first apartment (I could invite anyone over without having to abide by anyone's rules).
3. I was meeting more women and was starting to hang out in the city more often.

Right away I lost focus on what I really was supposed to be doing. I wasn't paying my bills on time and I started missing work a lot because I was partying all the time. I had no focus. All I was really doing was hurting myself, though, because the responsibilities I had could have helped prepare me for my future. But nothing meant more to me than the city life.

After only two months in my apartment, I ended up breaking my lease and leaving the rental property without giving notice. I couldn't afford the rent because of the poor decisions I had made and because of my inability to correctly prioritize my life. I had no sense of direction; I felt I was headed down the wrong path and there was no turning back. When I moved to Atlanta, I was only twenty-four years old and had no education and no real work or career history. The only thing I was determined to do was live the life I had always envisioned for myself—after all, I was at every club in town, talking to beautiful women and enjoying life, and that was the life I wanted all the time. But I didn't have much and I had to front like I was better. So I did what I knew best—I lied and manipulated women.

I started telling lie after lie to the women I met. I couldn't be honest for anything in the world. I used to see women attracted to men who drove nice cars and paid good money to get into the nicest and most elite clubs in the city. Because the women liked that, that's what I wanted to do. Even though I knew that, financially, I was not in a position to do that, I would still take my entire paycheck, which wasn't much, and spend it like I had plenty more to my name. And if it got the attention of a beautiful woman, I didn't care.

After some time I started to realize that this life was becoming too expensive for me, so I decided that I wanted to find a young lady to try and settle down with. That's when I came across this gorgeous sister named Erin. She was everything I was hoping to find in a woman. Erin was very caring and loving and she truly enjoyed being around me. The problem was that I knew that and played off of it. I knew I wanted her but because I was in this big city, I still wanted more. Erin was different than most of women with whom I normally associated myself. She was the type of woman who would motivate me and push me to be the best person I could be—something that I needed but didn't pay much attention to at the time. Her family embraced me and I started to see family like I had never seen it before. They were so close and I felt like this was the life I wanted, but I still couldn't remain focused enough to get it. And I only felt that I wanted that life when I was around her family. Unfortunately, I was too far gone and there was no turning back from my devious ways at that point.

After Erin and I had been together for a year, I began to notice myself becoming this controlling person. I was very spoiled and started acting very insecure around her. I knew it was wrong but I didn't care. I started to revert back to my childhood ways (this spoiled kid wanting things his way all the time). I could see that Erin was trying her hardest to put up with any wrongdoing, but it started to bother her way too much (like they say, when a woman is fed up there's nothing a man can do). After months of emotional abuse, Erin had had enough. Because of my controlling and determined ways, I would not let her go. When I realized I was really losing her, I noticed I started wanting to have a special bond with her even more. (Sometimes a person doesn't realize a good thing until it's gone.) I got so out of control and tried so hard to keep her from leaving that she had to involve her mother. After seeing that I knew I had gone too far. I had become this out-of-control young man who needed a serious reality check. After that relationship ended and I had healed emotionally, I started working very hard so that I would never be a control freak or a spoiled individual like that again. I wanted to become a great man and set an example of how to be respectful toward women. But of course that didn't happen in the least.

As I have said before, growing up, some of my behavior was influenced by what I saw around my neighborhood, whether it was my uncles, my brothers, or the average Joe I saw in the streets. But none of them had a worse effect on me than my cousin Jake. Jake had been living in Atlanta for a couple of years before I got there. He knew things about the city that if I would never have discovered on my own. He knew all the hottest spots and where the nicest girls hung out. After breaking up with Erin, I started hanging out with my cousin and we began to do the things I wanted to do when I got there—hanging out at the best clubs and chasing women.

My cousin got his kicks from meeting women and seeing just how many of them he could sleep with. His main statement to me was, "You are not trying to marry these hoes, just meet them and sleep with them." That was obviously something I had been doing for awhile, but I was really trying to change. And as long as I was with Jake, that was not going to happen. A lot of my bad behavior was influenced by my cousin. I would watch him tell women just about anything and they would believe it, time and time again. The difference between Jake and me was that he didn't have a job at all, but he would always dress nice. He would say to me, "Just because you don't have money doesn't mean you can't look like you got money." That was a technique I would use for many years.

After hanging with and learning from Jake, I would have women buy me things and pay off my debts for me. I would drive their cars, borrow money from them, and if I didn't have a place to stay I would stay with them. I was terrible—my word was no good and I was very inconsistent, but convincing. I didn't take the blame for anything I did wrong. But one thing I did have was a conscience. I knew the things I was doing were wrong, and sometimes I would get myself together and cut back on the partying for awhile, trying to calm down. But my surroundings—and by that I mean Jake—wouldn't let me off the hook. Jake had become a terrible influence on me. The more women I saw Jake with, the more women I wanted. It started to become a contest between us. I was trying my best to keep him from being able to claim that he had been with more women than I had. It was fun but it became pathetic after awhile. I started to feel bad about how I was treating these ladies. The more women I met, the more women got hurt.

Growing into a young man, I started to realize that I needed to make a change in my approach with women. I had to stop telling them only what they wanted to hear, knowing full well that I was lying. I also needed to stop trying to convince them that I was that special guy they were looking for; that just wasn't true. I started meeting established, successful women who only wanted a man who was honest with them. Because my life wasn't good and I didn't have anything to offer a woman but lies, when I met a mature woman who was very accomplished, I felt intimidated by her success. If I did have the courage to approach her it was only with lies, because I felt if my qualifications were not good enough, she wouldn't accept me. Why was it so hard for me to be myself?

1. I didn't have a college education.

2. Didn't have a good job.

3. I didn't even own a car.

I felt as if I couldn't compete with what the city had to offer. So I just lied my way into the lives of these ladies.

By the time a woman realized that my life was a lie, I'd already gotten what I wanted out of her—sex, money, and material things. It was very sad to me to see how a woman felt after being used. But what was even sadder was that I didn't even care. I was never going to see those women again. What I didn't know was that, with some of them, I had ruined their trust in men and was reinforcing the stereotype about men—that men are dogs and there are no good men out there. My attitude was that it wasn't my problem to fix and that the next man they'd come across could deal with it. I couldn't care less how they felt.

Then in 2002 I met Jennifer. Physically, this young lady had everything I desired in a woman. She had beautiful eyes, beautiful hair, a gorgeous smile, and—most of all—a nice body. I immediately wanted one thing from her, just as I did with many other women, but with her I got more—this woman had my nose wide open. All I wanted was to spend as much time with her as possible. Everything between us moved quickly. I really started forgetting my priorities. Jennifer was living with her parents and the majority of the time was spent together at their house. After about a week we had sex, and after that first time I was whipped. I started to think she was the one for me, but not in a true emotional way. She was beautiful, the sex was great, and that was all that mattered to me. I didn't spend time with anyone but this girl. I met her family within the first two weeks, I started hanging out with all of her friends and she even started spending nights at my place. I would do just about anything for this girl—I thought it was love at first sight.

Our relationship got to the point where I would ask her to have my baby in the middle of sex and she would respond, "Yes." She may have not really meant it, but I took her literally and proceeded to conceive that baby, despite the fact that we were not married and had no careers and no education. But what the heck, I didn't care. I was going to be with that girl and if it took a baby to make that happen, then so be it. A month later we found out that we were indeed having that baby. Jennifer cried, but I was overcome with joy. After a while of celebrating the fact that we had a baby on the way, reality hit me: How was I going to take care of a baby? Since I never had a father in my life, the only thing I could think of was how to stay in my child's life and not become like my own father.

During the pregnancy my focus shifted to the baby and my attention to Jennifer lessened. My womanizing ways also started to affect our relationship. The fact that she was pregnant with my baby made me realize she would now be in my life forever—at least, that's what I thought. Throughout the pregnancy I reverted back to being this controlling, insecure man who wanted all the attention and wanted things his way. I would pick fights with her, which stressed her out and made her not want to be around me. Around her parents we would act as if everything was great, but when we were alone together all hell would break loose. The more bad behavior I displayed, the further she pulled away. I could sense that her intentions were to have this baby and then get away from me. I would blame all of our problems on her. I felt myself becoming this terrible person. After months of behaving this way with her, not to mention that the baby was due soon, I decided I needed to become a different person. With the baby's arrival on the horizon and my focus being so out of place, I had no choice but to change. Being afraid that I was losing the woman who was carrying my child was an awful feeling for me. It never even crossed my mind that I could have easily asked Jennifer to marry me. That was just too much of a commitment that I couldn't handle. Marriage was never an option for me.

My son was born on September 8, 2003. I was the proudest man in the world. I named him after my oldest brother Michael, who helped me through so much in my life. Holding my son in my arms and at the same time thinking about how my life had been so far, I knew I needed to figure out how to fix my problems and make things right for him. I had a way with women that was extremely disrespectful. I'd treated them like they were trash. Did I deserve to even be with a woman, knowing that the only thing I was going to do was break her heart? The whole time, I was looking into my son's eyes as if he was really paying attention to me, listening to me as I made promises that I might not keep. But the healing process had begun.

Before I officially named my son, I had wanted to name him after me. But throughout the pregnancy I could only ask myself how I could give this boy the name of a selfish womanizer who disrespected women, had no goals, no career, and no education, and still want him to follow in my footsteps. It was a no-brainer to name him after my brother rather than myself. If I wanted my son to follow in my footsteps and if I wanted to be a positive role model for him, I was really going to have to change my ways and become a real man. My biggest fear was becoming a deadbeat dad who couldn't support his son or teach him how to become a decent, respectable man. I was convinced that my change would start immediately

The next year I attempted to go back to school as the first step toward changing myself. I enrolled at Atlanta Metropolitan College to pursue my childhood dream of becoming a basketball coach. Basketball was something that I had always excelled at and it was also something that really held my interest. But after two years of studies at AMC, I hit another obstacle.

1. I had used up all of my financial aid, so I had no money to finish my studies.

2. I was working at a job that didn't pay much, so I couldn't pay out of pocket for school.

So the only thing I could do was drop out once again to make ends meet for my son. It was either finish school or lose my job and not be able to take care of my son. Because I couldn't balance the two, the decision was easy for me: keep the job and take care of my son. But I still found myself facing a dilemma: the job was not paying me enough to support my child, not to mention I still had to support myself. What was I to do? I ended up getting a second job. What a waste that turned out to be, but as a man who had the responsibility to do right by his son, I did what had to be done so that I could provide for my child.

My second job was working as a janitor, but the entire time I held that job, I was thinking to myself that this was not the answer. Was this really God's intention for me? I was still making very little money, so I started borrowing money from my brother Michael, who already had to support his family. Because of all my bad decisions I was really headed in the wrong direction. And because of my situation, I had no other option but to hold onto that janitor job, which was only supposed to last for a month, for an entire year. Imagine having the opportunity to get a free education with a basketball scholarship, only to end up cleaning toilets for a living. What a waste of a potential man I had become.

After awhile, I began to lose hope again. When a man loses hope he loses ground, he loses faith, and I had neither. I didn't understand what having faith meant. When I was a kid we always hoped that we could have things; we always hope that we would get out of poverty because that's all we knew. Growing up poor the way I did, once I tasted a little bit of success I became accustomed to that finer lifestyle. I forgot my morals and values. I was lost. I had no guidance but Michael's. He did his best to try and keep me straight, but how much can you teach a grown man? He would always tell me that my lifestyle would catch up with me and that I needed to stop living above my means. Would I listen? Not even close. After so much struggle and pain I just knew I couldn't overcome, the street life began to call to me again. This pattern seems to always come back when I least expected it. Instead of trying to better myself, get an education, and learn the importance of life, my lust for women overtook me again. I found myself back at it again, this time the sad thing about it was:

1. I still had these jobs that weren't paying much at all.

2. I had a son to raise.

Instead of it being all about my son, it turned out to be all about me. I started putting my son second to my own needs and desires—the deadbeat dad started to become a reality. How could this be after all the promises I made to my son that I would always be there for him? Was my son now becoming subject to my lies? I started to ask myself if I was really a great father or if I was simply a sperm donor who helped create a baby that he couldn't raise. It's not like I was ever taught how to be a great dad—I'd never even met my own father. I never had the mindset of getting married because I had never seen a healthy marriage in my own family. What I do know is that kids need comforting. How could

I go about comforting my son when I couldn't comfort myself? At that point in my life I could not be an example to my son. I started thinking that maybe having a child was a mistake. My priorities were not where they needed to be. I started to make excuses and come up with lies that kept me away from my son. Weeks would go by without me seeing him. I would tell Jennifer lie after lie—"I have to work late," or "My car isn't running well." But yet when it was time to go to the club, I was ready at a moment's notice. It had become habit to me and it was easy because no matter what, I knew that my child's mother would always provide the nurturing that he needed. Like many fathers, it was easy for me to walk out of my child's life. I was running from responsibility. I would pick and choose when I would see my son. It was becoming pathetic and both sides of the family began to notice. I was the ultimate worst when it came to being a father. I was a disgrace. I had no one to turn to because no one trusted me. I had lied myself too far into a hole that I didn't even try to get myself out of it. After separating myself from my son, I felt there was no way I could gain back that trust. After years of disrespecting women, lying to my family, and spending weeks at a time away from my child, I knew I needed to change.

After separating from Jennifer, I became close to a young lady I worked with named Carrie. Carrie was not normally the kind of woman I would date—she wasn't really my type—but she was special in her own way. Since I never knew how to be a man, she really taught me the importance of being a great man in a relationship. Aside from Michael, Carrie was the only person who knew how to motivate me. She was so determined to do well that it rubbed off on me.

Carrie drove a nice luxury car and she owned several real estate properties, and she was willing to open that life up to me. I learned a lot from her. In the time that we dated, I learned the importance of straightening out my credit, saving money, and life how to project a positive image, something that I had never considered. But the most important thing she introduced me to was God. I never knew having faith and putting God first the way I learned from her. I started attending church with her on a regular basis and started reading the Bible. I made a dramatic turnaround because of this woman, whether she knew it or not.

Now with all of that done and me knowing the Lord a little more, there was one skill I still lacked, and that was how to be a boyfriend—a quality I had never be able to grasp. The way I felt with this woman was great. Things started happening that I would never have even dreamed about. I even experienced my first trip outside the U.S. with Carrie—we took a wonderful trip to the Bahamas together.

And since my credit was good I was able to get myself a nicer vehicle.

Everything was going great and I thought I had everything I'd always wanted. After all the success I had in that year, you would think I'd grown up some. God had been good to me and I had a great woman in my life. So what was the problem? Well, the problem was that I still lacked that knowledge of how to treat people who had been good to me. When I got my new car, I let it go to my head. I lost focus on my relationship with Carrie and our breakup was really difficult for me. I had never known how to deal with rejection, and this was the first time I had ever been heartbroken over a woman. I'd been disappointed with women before, but I'd never felt like I had just lost that special one.

The demise of that relationship led to my resolve to never again become deeply involved with a woman. Relationships to me at that point were slim to none; I couldn't care less about them, but I still wanted that sexual pleasure. Women were just a stepping stone for me. I had nothing to lose. I was never going to be hurt again. My goal was to break their hearts before they broke mine. It got so bad that women couldn't figure me out, and it became a joke to me. I'd be this charming, warm-hearted man who women fell for instantly, and then I would turn into a nightmare, constantly playing mind games with them. You would think since I grew up with a single mother and had only one sister that my attitude toward women would be better and more respectful, but it never was. I also never thought one woman who broke my heart would have that much affect on how I treated the next woman, but she did. But did I ever think that the way I was treating her was wrong? Did I ever think that I was hurting her feelings? No, because I was selfish. Remember, all my life it was always about me, and only me. I never grew out of that need for attention. It's so disappointing to see someone give you their heart only for you to stomp all over it. That's exactly what I was doing and I didn't have a care in the world. If I was going to live this life then I was going to take advantage of it—what an attitude to have. Just as they say women sometimes use what they got to get what they want, I would think, "Here I am, this handsome young man that women like and are attracted to—why I don't do the same?" So that's exactly what I did. I had to figure out how to get to the top, so I started using women more and more, making them think we were in a relationship and then end it once I had gotten what I wanted from them. I had become this great big scum of the earth. It became clear to me that time was passing me by and my life was not going to get any better. The only thing I had going for me was good looks and a great talk game, or rather, a great lying game. Would I ever learn my lesson and become a great man? Would I ever be in a committed relationship? It felt as if the answer was no, but was that what I really wanted?

One thing that I do know is that in order to love someone else you have to love yourself. And the most important thing is to love God first. I never knew how to love myself, so I could never love another woman. Throughout my life I had treated women like they were nothing, like they were beneath me, because I didn't love myself, nor did I have the relationship with God that I should have been seeking. The only time I even remember going to church was when I was dating Carrie. When I was on my own I would never wake up and say, "Hey, I'm going to find a church home and try to become a better person." If I met a woman and she went to church I would ask her if I could go to church with her. And then I would brag about the times I did go to church only to gain her approval. I would become this godly man overnight and make her think I was really into church. Now if that's not one step from hell I don't know what is. But it was so easy for me to do.

I was too far gone. My infidelities in relationships were a must-have, and no relationship was going to work if it was left solely up to me. There was no turning back; I had already accepted the fact that I had no career and no goals, so I was going to ruin many lives as possible.

I had every excuse in the world not to better myself. As long as I was making a little money and what little bills I had were being paid, I couldn't care less if my life made a dramatic turnaround. I was paying child support now, thinking that I was taking care of my child, adjusting my wages and realizing that after child support was paid I still had enough left to live and hang out at night. It started getting so bad for me that paycheck-to-paycheck living was not even good enough. Month after month, week after week, I accrued more debt because I was still living above my means. I was in a no-win situation. Child support had to be paid and I still had to live. Now even if I wanted a woman I couldn't have one. Not only was I not respectable enough to have one trust me but financially I was below sea level. I was becoming desperate. I had nowhere to turn. It got to the point where I didn't even care about my life anymore. It was just as if I was that kid again, always trying to get attention. I felt as if no one cared about me. I was in Atlanta, this big city, where I couldn't call on anyone for help because of my lack of credibility. What was I to do but start feeling sorry for myself? I started living in the past. My excitement then started coming from me trying to fool not only myself, but others, too, that I was this great person and did all these great things. But no one cared because they knew the life I was talking about didn't exist. When people would ask me about my life I would always refer them back to my early years as if I were still living that life. Living in the past was the one thing that brought me joy. I had become a big joke to myself, and was unreliable to my family—not even they could trust the things that I said. I was giving up on life.

What is the purpose of a man? Growing up I thought I knew. To be honest, I thought I knew it all. But I didn't know anything. The most I knew was that a man is to have a job, support his family, and just live life to the fullest. And I thought, in my situation, one out of three wasn't bad. My idea was to live life to the fullest and grab every opportunity to do what it took to be happy, which is some cases wouldn't always be the right thing to do. But that was the only thing I did. I forgot about the real essence of life and about how to respect the people in my life and how to set an example of a real man. Growing up, I never knew my father and I never really knew God—the only thing I had was my family. You would think that family would be all I needed. Maybe that's true in some situations or in some people's lives, but my family was different. We were never close like the families in our neighborhood. We never went to church together; we never sat at the table to have dinner together like a family should. We never had reunions with our extended family. We were just a family who made the best of what we had. What did I learn from this? I never recall my mother coming to school to check on me or even coming to my sporting events. The sad thing about my mom was that she never signed me up for anything that would keep me involved and out of trouble. I had to learn how to manage and create happiness on my own. How large a role did that play in my growth and development? I never interacted with people well enough to keep friends. All in all, I wasn't a great person.

I didn't know how to deal with the fact that other people had feelings, too. That was not my concern. All that mattered to me was that I got what I wanted. So to me, at this point in my adult life, the purpose of a man was to simply survive. But what was I surviving? I had nothing I could really call my own. If I were to ever meet a great woman, I had nothing to offer her. What woman would want a man with no goals, no motivation, no respect for his surroundings, no education, and most of all, one who didn't understand what it took to be a man. Sometimes I would ask myself why I was even alive. Here I was, this man who'd had so many opportunities to finish school, play the sport that he loved, and have a great life. What was the problem? Why was I still in a deep hole? I lacked focus and ambition. I was always running. I thought it was too much work to look for a solution to my problems—it seemed like a waste of time. I had thrown away every opportunity I'd had that could've kept me from getting me in the dump I found myself in.

When a man starts feeling bad for himself he becomes hopeless. I was that man. I couldn't care less about what was happening to me or what people thought of me. I was at the lowest point of my life. But when people saw me they couldn't tell I had any problems that need attention; I hid it so well. I had never really trusted any woman growing up. If I had, maybe my life would have been easier. Maybe I would have been married by now, raising a great family and being a decent, hard-working man. But that wasn't the reality of my situation.

A Gentleman's Cry

The Woman I Admire

Chapter 8

The Woman I Admire

Everyone has that special person whom they truly care about and miss when they are gone. If that's the case, tell the one you love how much you love them and care for them while they are still here. It's a shame how many people wait until it's too late to say how they really feel about someone. Never be ashamed to tell someone how you feel, because you never know when it will be the last time.

The only woman I ever felt I could trust was my grandmother—what a sweet woman she was. I would do anything and everything for her. No one had a better relationship with my grandmother than I did. I remember how she would get up early in the morning, make us breakfast, dress us for the day, and then we would all go out to work in the garden she had planted in her backyard. Sometimes I would get up early with her most days before my siblings woke up and help her in the garden myself. I would pull weeds, feed the chickens and the dogs, and help her fertilize and water the garden. I learned everything about how to tend a garden; I had a daily lesson.

Sometimes my grandmother would send us to the neighborhood grocery store for her. She would write down on a list all the things she needed from the store and give the list to my older brother because she thought I would lose it. I would get upset every time, but she had this way of involving me so that I would feel like I was contributing. She would ask me to check off the items on the list as my brother picked them up. I felt very important. When we would get back home she would have these huge white buckets full of peas and corn, and she would ask us to shuck the vegetables into a pot. That was the only thing I didn't like because it generally became an all-day thing. But it was for my grandmother, so I agreed. I remember having all this hair on my head, and my grandmother would sit me down on her lap and braid my hair. I didn't really like it because the neighborhood kids would pick on me and call me a girl. I would run back to the porch and ask her to take the braids out because my friends were making fun of me. But once again, my grandmother always had her way of making me feel good. She would tell me that those kids were not my friends; real friends wouldn't pick on me. That always made me feel better and I would soon be up and back out the door to play with my friends again.

I never saw my grandmother upset. She didn't have one angry bone in her body. She would open up the door to any of the other kids in the neighborhood and feed them. The only bad thing I do remember was the way my uncles acted around her. Boy, they were terrible. They ate up everything in the house, always borrowed money from my grandmother and never paid her back, and they never cleaned up after themselves—they expected my grandmother to do it. They would come into the house at all hours of the night, and they would even fight with each other around her. I really hated that, but I couldn't say anything because they would whip me when my grandmother wasn't looking (she would have none of that). She would always tell me, "Do not grow up to be like your uncles. Theirs is an example you should not follow. When you grow up, do the complete opposite." My uncles were a bad influence on me. They would do drugs in the house, and sometimes even have the nerve to bring women home—though I didn't mind the girls because I would sneak around and see what they were doing.

After several years I really started to notice changes in my grandmother's health. She began walking differently and I didn't know why, but it was very strange to me. I also noticed her starting to depend on others more. But she still had that fight in her. She went from her walking around on her own to walking with a cane. I would insist on helping her but she would always respond that she didn't need my help. The only thing she would let me do was to get the door for her. Since she was unable to move around like she used to, it was also strange to not see her getting out of bed later than she used to.

As I grew up I stopped going to see my grandmother as often as I did when I was a kid. Granted, I was getting older and I was experiencing more things, but I would still check in on her from time to time, to see how she was doing. After awhile coming around sometimes turned into not visiting at all. I realized that I spent a lot of time around my grandmother, and it was all about me now. Living in the same hometown, you would think that a grandson would make it a point to see his grandmother on a regular basis; well, I was only visiting about once every three months. I didn't know what type of an effect that had on her but it was probably disappointing. But being a young, active kid in the streets, that didn't really concern me. As long as I didn't hear that she was doing badly and if she hadn't called on me to come by to do her a favor, I figured she was doing just fine. I wasn't worried about her in the slightest.

Several years passed, I was older and hadn't seen my grandmother in awhile, so she began to cross my mind from time to time. Since I wasn't busy anymore, I had some time to visit her. When I got to her house I really noticed a change in her. She looked at me and the first thing came out of her mouth was, "Boy, where you been? I've been asking about you. Why haven't you been by to see me?" I told her that I had been away at college. What? I couldn't believe that I just lied to my grandmother. I mean, that lie was so easy, and seeing how it made her feel I couldn't tell her the truth, which was that I had dropped out of school and had no plans to return. She was so happy thinking I was in school and on my way to being better than my uncles, and she was proud—so I ran with it.

At this time my grandma wasn't even able to walk. She was confined to this chair, where she would sit all day. Sometimes she would even sleep in the chair. I felt devastated seeing her that run-down, but I didn't want her to know how I felt—I didn't want to make her feel bad (one thing about her was that her spirits were always up). My siblings and I didn't visit her as often as when we were younger, but it didn't bother her. It was as if she had become a loner, like no one cared to see her. We did, it was just that other things had become more important to us than her. You would think that I would want to spend more time around this beautiful woman who had such a great heart and who had done so much for me—it should've been a no-brainer. But I continued to do what I thought was best for me and only visit her when I decided I had the time.

It was 2002 and I had been away from Statesboro for a year. I hadn't seen my grandmother in years. I'd made a few visits here and there, but they were few and far between. I was convinced that my grandmother was alright and that I didn't need to worry. Then one day when I was heading up the street to catch the bus to go to work, my cell phone rang. It was my brother telling me something that I never thought I would hear—the call that no one ever wants to receive:

> "Hey man, what's up?"
>
> "Nothing, I'm headed to work."
>
> "Well I'm calling you to let you know that Mama"—that's what we called her—"is gone."
>
> "What do you mean, gone," I replied
>
> "She passed away."

Damn, my mouth dropped and I couldn't believe it. I hadn't seen this woman in a long time and the first thing I thought of was the lie I told her about me being in college. I felt really, really bad. There was no way I was going to shake this off my conscience. I was devastated. Pile my grandmother's death on top of everything that was going on in my life, and I really turned into a man with no purpose. This was the woman who raised me, for all intents and purposes, and I couldn't even make time to visit her on a regular basis. What kind of man was I? I couldn't tell my own grandmother who raised me that I loved her for everything she had done? In August of 2002 we buried my grandmother, and all I could think about was how my last words to her were a lie. How could I ever tell anyone I loved them if I couldn't even tell my own grandmother? I miss her dearly, but I know she's in a better place now.

They say only a father can raise a boy to become a man. Well, in my case, the values I did learn came from my grandmother. Now I think about all the little things we did together when I was young, from waking up early in the morning to start the day to planting a garden, taking out the trash, and learning to clean up after myself. My grandmother worked so hard to strengthen my character and teach me to work well with others—these were the tasks that would carry me through life, if I would let them. Those lessons may have been simple, but they were of the utmost importance when it came to living life to the fullest. She knew full well that I was a kid who needed extra attention and was a straight menace, but she was always working to groom me into a decent young man, a man who would know the importance of life and how to handle certain situations. You don't think about that much when you are a kid, but life becomes a boomerang and what you lack in life always comes back around to give you the reality check you need. My grandmother did the very best she could with me and all I had to do was soak it in and follow those little rules; it wasn't a hard thing to do, but I just couldn't grasp it and live like she wanted me too. I constantly challenged her morals, as if I was right and she was wrong. I fought everything that may have been right for me because I felt that my way was always the right way. She offered me words of wisdom and the only thing she wanted me to do was follow her morals and try to understand the value of life. Not only did I fail that test, but I failed myself as a person. There was no way out for me.

A Gentleman's Cry

Sorting Through Life's Priorities

Chapter 9

Sorting Through Life's Priorities

"Never put off for tomorrow what you can do today. Tomorrow is never promised to you. Remember always that if you play now you will suffer later. Always put your responsibilities first and everything else will follow. You may think you have everything you want until something you needs come along."

~D. Taylor

Why am I so afraid of commitment? Why am I afraid of a good woman? I asked myself these questions over and over again. Do I even deserve to be with a classy, successful woman? Here I was, this single man with a son to raise and nothing to call my own. I had nothing to show for my life but memories of a great time I had hanging in the streets. Who was I fooling? I had become so obsessed with material things that I assumed that I had to have those things in order to find that special woman. I was very simple-minded and only looked at life through the lens of material things. I wanted the nice car, the finest girl, and all the perks that came with that lifestyle. But the more I tried to get those things the further behind I got in my true priorities. I got so caught up in that lifestyle that I forgot how to really be a man. So what type of woman was I seeking? I didn't want a spiritual woman or a woman of great morals—it was all about appearance.

I didn't care about her intellect or what she had going for herself, the only thing that mattered to me was that she looked good and that other men would be envious of me for having her.

The girls I was interested in were, like me, all about money and material things. But that was something I didn't care about. The little money that I did have I spent on those women like I was a baller. I couldn't save money to save my life. I was always out having a great time and enjoying what I thought was good for me. When I did meet a woman I liked, I fronted like I had everything in the world. But I was living this fantasy lifestyle that I could only front for a little while. I related everything about myself to finances when I would meet a woman I wanted. It was all about where she wanted me to take her and what I could do for her. I never considered that this might not be what she wanted, but if I was stupid enough to blow my money on her, then she wasn't going to stop me. And when the funds ran out, she ran out. I couldn't live the life I promised her.

I lied about the smallest things, not thinking that I would have to live that lie for the duration of the relationship. I was basically living life like a movie script: Boy meets girl, boy lies to girl, loses girl, and then moves on. It was a pattern. I had gotten so bad that soon, women could immediately tell what I was all about as soon as they met me. I was this loud, arrogant man who had a little boy's mentality. I became an easy target for women who wanted someone to spend money on them because I made it so obvious that I would do just that. Sometimes I would even think that those women really liked me for who I was—that's how pathetic I had become. The game I thought I had at one point turned out to be a disqualification. I was learning a lesson: how to blow my money. It turned out that the games I used to play on women backfired and were now being played on me. My brother used to always say, "Man, what type of women do you mess with?" I would quickly respond that the women I messed with did everything for me. But he knew I was lying, because I could never keep any money on me; I was always broke. Hell, I would even ask him for money to take these women out. I had lost all self-respect. I thought the only way to get a decent, classy woman was to have a lot of money. I wanted that lifestyle and I was determined to get it. But I had run out of options. I knew I had some soul-searching to do to figure out a way to turn my life around. I knew I needed to make some changes quickly; it wasn't all about me anymore.

My motto in life had become "Whatever happens, happens!" I figured at that point in my life, what else could possibly go wrong? How many more people could I hurt? Who could even trust me? I had no more money to spend on girls, and no money to help me enjoy my life. At this point, what else could I possibly do? Everything revolved around reconstructing my life and how I was going to go about it. I was afraid to tell anyone the truth about myself. I was afraid to even push myself to do better because of my fear of giving up and losing control over my life. I had to realize that my past was not my future. I had to finally face reality and admit to the fact that I had a serious ego problem and a problem with dishonesty and admitting that I didn't know everything that life had in store for me. Only when I could admit that could I become a great man who could be trusted again.

I had no clear image of a real man. I was confused about how to be responsible. If things did not directly benefit me, then I wanted no part in them. I used to hear the saying, "You learn from your mistake and you move on." Well, I always moved on but I never learned from my mistakes. How could a man move on when he doesn't have any focus? I began to think that, no matter what I did, I was always going to be stuck in the life I had made for myself. I thought I would never be able to have a family of my own and that I would never be successful in anything. I was never the type of man to think about his future. For me, it was living in the moment, and my moment was going to be hanging out at the hottest clubs and being with the prettiest women. That's all I knew and I didn't think any of that was going to change.

Men today have to step it up a notch. We can't have our strong men not taking responsibility for their actions. A man is every bit the leader of his house. A woman seeks a strong man, a man who is a caring provider and a leader. How does a man assume these roles? The most important thing to know is that a man has to have God in his life. God is the answer to all problems. A man who seeks God is a man who can lead his family in the right direction. What does a man expect from a woman? Well, a man of God seeks a supportive woman who is warm and understands how to let a man be a man, a woman who knows how to raise her children to be good, kind-hearted human beings who respects the family unit. Men have to understand how to be a role model for their children, because kids look to their father for guidance and support. A man should always stay strong for his family, stand tall, and accept the fact that he can be dedicated. No matter what the circumstances if a man has God in his life and is faithful to his family, nothing can tear that family apart. A man should set an example for his kids so that they always know they can count on him. A real man admits his faults, and looks for ways to resolve his problems. And no matter what, a man has to stay dedicated to his family and always put their needs ahead of his own. A positive home is always a happy home. A man should never put anything before his family. And the most important thing for a man is to live God's word to the fullest.

After all the adversity I faced, and having no one to turn to, my life began to get darker and darker. I treated women poorly, I had lied to just about everyone who had tried to help me, and I lost the one woman I could trust—what was I to do now? The answer was easy enough: seek God. But like most advice I'd ever received, it went in one ear and straight out the other. I had no intention of seeking God. I didn't even know how to go about it. When I did go to church, my body was there but my mind sure wasn't. I could hear the pastor talking about God's Word, but I could never comprehend any of it. I didn't understand what some of the Word meant or what purpose it served me. I was only at church so I could say I went—I wasn't learning a damn thing. I could see how people reacted to certain messages, how they would jump to their feet and praise the Lord, but it was just funny to me. I never volunteered to help the church. To be honest I never even had a home church. I would bounce around from church to church, hoping that I would gain some kind of understanding. Reading the Bible was never an option for me.

The only time I ever picked up the Bible was when I knew I would be going to church. Things were going so badly for me that I even started to question God's existence. If there really was a God, then why was I struggling with so much? Why was I treating people so poorly? I was lying, cheating, and being this nasty person with a huge ego problem and no respect for anyone. I knew the word of God but didn't know God himself. I had no faith, so why should I even bother to seek Him?

Church was never an integral part of my life growing up, and I had made it this far, so why should I get to know God now? What changes could he possibly make in my life? Whenever people would talk about the Lord around me, I would always come up with excuses and get very defensive—I didn't want to hear that stuff. It didn't help, either, to have a family that always talked about the church but didn't actively try to live a godly life. How could I trust their word? They were nothing but hypocrites to me. They would talk about their feelings about God and the church, and then we would immediately go back to chasing girls and getting our drink on. That's all I knew. That careless, partying lifestyle was the only thing that was important to me. When I went to church my only objective was to see what type of women were there and what they were wearing. I was just an extra body, taking up space.

After several months of trying to fit in at church, I just gave up altogether. I wouldn't think about church for weeks. Then weeks turned into months and months turned into years. I was convinced that nothing could turn my life around. I didn't affiliate myself with church-going people—I didn't want that lifestyle to rub off on me. I stopped believing in faith and hope, and the less I heard about it, the better. I used to hear all the time that prayer is power and can help you with everything if you just believe. Well, I tried that and none of my prayers were answered, at least not in the way that I thought they should've been. I never understood that you had to be careful what you ask for, because you may get exactly what you ask for. And I was getting all the wrong things—things that were only dragging me further down into a void.

Nothing seemed to get better for me. People started to ask me, "Why are you single? And what do you do in your free time?" My answer would be, "I'm not looking for a woman and I do absolutely nothing in my spare time." I started not wanting anyone in my life. I was so content to be alone that when the weekends would arrive, I would just lock myself away in my apartment, without even trying to see friends or family. Of course, it wasn't that I didn't want people in my life, I just didn't want to lie to them anymore and I didn't know how to stop. I had begun to try to figure out who I was as a person and stop blaming my problems on everybody else. And I knew that until I figured that out there was no way I could let myself get involved with or be around anyone. I became this quiet person who didn't say much. Most people assumed I was being self-centered and thought of me as thinking that I was all that. I knew that wasn't what I was doing, but I didn't bother to correct anyone.

What was I accomplishing by being so alone? I really never had any friends. My brother and cousin were pretty much the only people to whom I was close enough to want to visit. There were times when I would try to just get away from my family for awhile, but they were what I really needed; they understood me best. I could take advice from them and accept the fact that they knew better than I did what was best for me. I had no direction and I was just taking life as it came. Life had become a no-win situation to me, and at times I didn't want to be alive anymore—I just wanted to give up. I was a total mess of a human being. How was I ever going to shake my problems? I was always in denial, never regaining focus and never believing in myself. I was only thinking about my past and wondering if living that life was the only thing I was born to do. Never knowing whom my father was, I started to wonder if maybe I had inherited my bad traits from him. I had no way of knowing. Who could I relate my problems to? I use to blame everything I went through on anyone besides myself. I never even tried to better myself. I could make my life appear to be a blessing to others, but in reality that was a coverup of who I really was. When things would get a little better, I would quickly forget how I got that far and have a total relapse. My lust for women was all that really mattered to me. Being with a woman was my sanctuary—not for the emotional relationship, but only for the physical aspect. Money and women were my sole focus.

My family could see the dramatic change in my life. Any help they tried to give me I took for granted. I was this grown man and I thought I had it going on. But I started to notice I was quickly falling back into bad habits from my teenage years. At one point, I had stopped drinking as much and wasn't really hanging out because I started to see the pattern of bad behavior that I once couldn't shake creeping back into my life. So I started to think things were good enough, and that I was fine again. But I was the type of person who couldn't sit still long enough to gather my thoughts. I wasn't even trying to better myself as a man. And instead of turning to my family for help I turned back to the thing I knew best: the streets. I felt comfortable hanging out late at night. It was freedom to me. Eventually I became a regular in the party crowd again—nothing too fancy; I tried to keep it on the lower-budget side of things. I would only go to places that I knew I could afford. But I would still blow five hundred dollars in one night at one club. Knowing that was all the money I had, I still didn't hesitate. I was always telling myself that money comes and goes, not thinking that I had bills to pay—and I don't even want to mention my bills. I would always come up with some excuse for why I couldn't pay a certain bill on time. I would repeatedly call the electric company to request an extension, just so I could have money for the nightlife. My priorities were so jacked up that I would rather go to the club before I paid my bills. I would even be late on paying my rent sometimes, just so I could have some fun. I had no idea how deep of a hole I was digging for myself. When I needed money I would ask my brother if I could borrow some from him. I knew I could always count on Michael to deliver for me. I would tell him that I needed to pay a bill by a certain day or they were going to turn my lights off, or that my rent was going to be late and I was going to be evicted if I didn't pay. Sometimes it worked and sometimes it didn't. But when it worked the money I would immediately call my cousin—who himself didn't have any money—and say to him, "Let's do it again," meaning "Let's get into the streets and spend the ten or twenty dollars I just got from my brother." Knowing that my brother was going to be there for me, I just knew I could spend that money and that I would still be alright when I needed more.

By the time my bills were due I never had money left to pay them, and off went my lights or my heat. Having a place to live is one thing, but having a place you can't afford is another. I lived in places I knew I couldn't afford because I was trying to impress people who couldn't really care less what I had. I thought that's what they expected, and to me it was a big deal. Life is all about the choices you make, and I chose to live like I was the man, but on a budget that couldn't pay for anything. I was that guy who would sit at home watching BET, wanting to make everyone think that I was everything I saw on those shows. I was a grown man physically, but a young boy at heart. Having a son to take care of was important to me but I didn't seem to know how to actually be a father to him. I would see my son when I could—only after I had no money to throw away at the clubs, and therefore no money to spend on him. What was I turning into? How could I shake this demon from my soul? Who could I turn to for help?

Things got more confusing by the day. My problem was that all my life, all I wanted was attention. Everything had to be my way. I was spoiled, I wanted respect, I lacked focus, and I was out of control. I didn't know how to talk to people. I could never get along with anyone except my family. And even then I had to work extremely hard to gain their trust. I was a wreck. I couldn't have a successful relationship because I was never honest with women. And I had never made any real friends. It was like people figured out what type of person I was as soon as we met. I had no inner peace and I wasn't a man of God, nor did I even believe or have faith that things could get better. My mother was only three hours away, but I never visited her as often as I should have. Whenever birthdays and holidays would come around I was so broke that I couldn't get anyone a gift. I became a ghost during those times. (Actually, that was the easiest thing about my life—

that I was able to disappear when it came time to celebrate other peoples' lives.)

I was a straight user and a leech, and I tried my best to suck everything I could out of people. I remember working with this older lady and not having enough money to pay my rent. I begged and promised her that if she gave me three hundred dollars I would pay her back. I never thought that I was capable of taking advantage of a sweet old woman like that, but I dodged and dodged this woman until she saw that I had no intention of paying her back. I was so disgusted with myself. I had become a disgrace to her and I wanted to quit the job. At that point, all I could think about was how my uncles took advantage of my grandmother in that same way—borrowing money and never repaying her. I had to do something. Later that year I started to give her ten dollars here and there until she finally told me to just keep the money. Then I found out she had stopped working at that job. To me that was like winning the battle, but what battle did I really win? All I knew was how selfish of me it was to take advantage of a woman who was so sweet and who had the decency to believe in me. I vowed then to never hurt anyone again and to try and seek help for myself. Sometimes I would get extremely stressed out because I couldn't fight the overwhelming emotions that I had. I was fighting a demon I couldn't defeat—myself. I began to reject my life. Then I realized that my poor decisions and my bleak outlook on life were affecting my performance at work. It became clear to me that I was in a no-win situation; I had too many negative things going on. I'd always had a little bit of sense, so I started wondering where I went wrong. Where did all of this begin?

A Gentleman's Cry

My Brother's Keeper: My Role Model

Chapter 10

My Brother's Keeper: My Role Model

> *Everybody has a role model within themselves. Search your soul to be the best role model for yourself and others will follow. Serve as an example of transformation as you journey through your life. If you choose to follow the example of another, make sure the steps you follow are those of a true and honest individual.*

Every child grows up either having a role model or at least wanting one. For me that person was Michael. He was the type of guy who did what it took to survive. To some kids, growing up in poverty seems like a failure; to Michael it was pure motivation—something that I was sorely lacking. Out of four boys in the house, it would seem reasonable to think that at least one of them would try to make something of themselves and work to set an example for the rest—well, that was Michael. My mother spoiled both my younger brother Tony and me so much that she hardly paid any attention to the rest of her kids. Her time was usually so devoted to the two of us that she often didn't even notice when the rest of my siblings were outside getting into trouble—and if she did notice, most of the time she wouldn't care.

Michael had a good head on his shoulders and he knew he had to fend for himself. He would find different jobs to do around our neighborhood so that he could work and make money to buy himself some clothes and food. He essentially maintained and supported himself from a very young age. He never got the kind of help from our mother that I received; the two of them were estranged. Eventually, it got to the point where he just stopped coming home most days. He had learned how to be a man when he was still a boy. We had no money and sometimes we had no food. Michael knew that and he often used the money he made to help feed me and Tony. Did we appreciate this help? Sometimes we did, but we took it for granted most of the time.

I remember seeing Michael and his friends get picked up by a white man in a big white pickup truck every day, and wondering where they were going. Then, every Friday afternoon he would show me at least two hundred dollars that he had earned from leaving everyday with this man. "Man," I would say, "What are y'all doing and how can I get money like that?" My brother had a way of getting what he wanted because he was such a likeable person; I, on the other hand, got along with hardly anyone. But my brother talked the man into letting me work with them anyway. As we headed to the rural side of town I started to see huge fields full of tomatoes, corn, and many other kinds of vegetables. We would jump off the back of the truck and work in these big fields. Picture that: black kids on the back of a white man's truck being dropped off in these fields full of vegetables and tobacco plants—it reminded me of slavery! I'm joking, of course. In actuality our situation couldn't have been further from that. The white man we worked for was a very nice old man. He would give us meals throughout the day as we worked. Honestly, the only downside to this deal was how hot it was sometimes.

After one week I enjoyed my first paycheck. Making my own money was a great feeling. Each week the amount would range from one hundred to one hundred and fifty dollars. I was making some good money for being so young but, unlike my brother, I had to give my money to my mother because I was too young to even cash a check. She would cash the check and give me about twenty dollars to spend for myself. My mother loved money—it was her paradise. I was always the same way, and I think I picked that characteristic up from my mother. Like me, she was not very good at managing her money. My brother, on the other hand, saved just about every penny he earned. If I'd had half the knowledge and sense that he had, I would have become a much better man. I had plenty of opportunities to be like my brother, but I never took advantage of them. I watched him turn into this great man with goals and direction that helped him keep his head above water, and although he had two other brothers he would always make time to try and teach me everything he knew. And just like him, I was very good at sports, which helped us create an even closer bond. Whatever sport he played, I played. I could tell my other brothers felt that it was unfair for him to spend so much time with me and not them, but I didn't care. I felt like I was really important to Michael, and that was something I desperately needed as a young boy. I thought I was going to be just like him.

Years later when Michael went off to college, I was left at home, trying to follow in his footsteps—something I was never able to do. I had all this knowledge that he had passed on to me, and I thought it would be easy to live up to the example he set. But the truth was, once he left and was out of my daily life, I took a turn for the worst. It became evident that I didn't have the heart or the determination that he possessed. It turned out that I really needed him around to motivate me to really work to live up to the expectations he had for me.

People started to tell me that I would never be like my brother, and that I would never make a name for myself. People always related to me as "the little brother." They would never say my name; they would just call me "little brother." I began feeling like my brother's shoes were too big to fill—his footsteps were overwhelming to me. I stopped working hard and no longer pushed myself to do my best. I became just another guy who took life for granted. I didn't see any reason to try to get the respect of others. I was quickly becoming a lazy person, wasting my potential without a care in the world. Life began to move in slow motion; everything I started only got half done. I was rarely asked to be a part of something because everyone knew I wasn't going to give my best effort to anything. When it came time to go to basketball camp with my team, I wasn't allowed to participate. No one believed in me. No one could trust my word.

All of this caused me to lose respect for myself. The only time I tried at anything was when the outcome would be directly beneficial to me. So, either I had to start making changes in my life or just stop putting myself in any situation that required even a small amount of accountability and essentially just give up. When Michael was on break from college he would call to check up on me, and every time he did I lied to him and told him everything was going well—and that was the easy part. I acted like he didn't know the truth about me already, forgetting that my brother was a household name in our hometown. He had ways of finding out just about anything he wanted to know about anyone in town. When I would tell him those lies he would just get quiet and then start laughing at me as if I were a joke. He would always say one line that I knew meant that he knew the truth: "Man, are you kidding me?" My response was always the same: "What?"—as if I was totally innocent and didn't know what he meant.

I started to think my brother had given up on me. The goals he set for me I would never reach or take seriously. I had messed up so many lives that my word could not be trusted. The only person who did anything to provide for me was my brother. It seemed like I was screaming for help every single day, and I couldn't turn to the friends I had at the time. (And of course, my mother was in no position to help me with anything.) I kept hearing, "Do something for YOU." But what could I do for myself? I had no sense of humor and no will to do anything that took effort. I always depended on others to do everything for me. I was always begging my friends and family for money, promising to pay them back, when I knew the entire time that I had no intention of doing so. Friends and family would see me coming and shut their doors in my face. If you asked anyone whether I was a reliable person, the answer would unquestionably be no. A man who can't be trusted is a man who has no knowledge of faith or the sense of what it takes to be responsible toward anything or anyone. It was sometimes better if everyone just left me alone to try to find the answers for myself. But what did it take to do that, and how or where could I do this? I would always ask my brother those questions. I listened very hard and tried to follow the instructions he gave me. They motivated me; Michael's answers were words for me to live by. I would soak them in like a sponge until our phone call ended. But reality would always fall back into my lap. And after awhile, my brother would just give up on me.

A Gentleman's Cry

My Testimony

Chapter 11

My Testimony

How much struggle must a young man encounter before he starts trying to figure out his life? For me, it took a mountain of strife. And the fact of the matter is that I never really figured things out. I was always searching for answers. I began to see that I'd had everything pretty much given to me, only for me to throw it away. Had I been able to appreciate the opportunities I'd had, I would have been in a much better situation. But I never knew how to sacrifice. I couldn't learn how to live without the things that I wanted. I didn't know how to adapt to certain situations. I was the boy who always had to get what he wanted, no matter what. Whatever the situation was, there had to be something in it for me; I couldn't waste my time on anything else. I was lazy and never helped my mother around the house. Bringing joy to peoples' hearts was not my issue. I'd had numerous opportunities to better peoples' lives just by helping them in a time of need, and I had ignored those chances. The problems people around me were having were not mine to deal with, but I would always make my problems theirs. I was sneaky and very persistent; I could slither my way into certain situations. My happiness stood second to nothing. The only thing I'd ever challenged myself with was getting what I wanted out of people, and that was the only goal I'd ever reached. I thought I was fooling people with my tactics. But the only person I was really fooling was myself. Had I learned that earlier in life, I might have been a more positive role model for those around me.

I've had sex with more than a hundred women in my life. And sleeping with them was one thing, but the big problem was the many of these women with whom I actually had unprotected sex. I started to think about how many of these women might have had a disease of some sort. That thought devastated me and I knew I had to get tested. In that moment I vowed to myself that I would never have unprotected sex with a woman again until I was married. That was a sobering moment for me, and it really changed my life. After carrying the thought of disease around on my conscience for months, I finally summoned up the nerve to take action and get myself tested. During a routine physical, the doctor asked me if I wanted a test. I declined at first, but deep down I knew that if I was going to one day have a successful relationship with a woman, this was something that needed to be done. I had to know my status. I took the test and after a few stressful days full of thoughts of what my life would be like if I had a disease, I received my results: they were negative. Thank God!

Why did I just offer that testimony? There are many people out there just like me who could easily be affecting other people's lives by spreading diseases they might not know they have. By the grace of God, everything I've been through turned out to work in my favor, though at times that was hard to see. My faith in God was never strong until I received my results of the test, and that's when I seriously vowed to make a real change. I'd never been in love with a woman and that was something I was slowly starting to search for in my life. I knew God had given me a second chance to become that kind of man.

Eventually, I found a home church with a strong, close-knit community. I fully believe that through God anything is possible. It was God who helped me begin my search for answers as to why I did such terrible things to the women in my life. I always wondered why I was this unhappy, constantly depressed person. Through God the answer became perfectly clear to me: I didn't love myself enough to even begin to love anyone else. I cheated myself, so I cheated others. I didn't respect myself, so I didn't respect others. I controlled women and preyed on their weaknesses. If a woman tried to do me some good I chased her away; if a woman tried to stand up to me I kicked her out of my life—I didn't want a challenge. It was too much work for me and I figured I didn't have the time to deal with that sort of thing.

Through my walk with God I have learned to be more patient with women. I learned to give them the respect that they deserve. They say that a woman is the backbone and the emotional center of a family, and that women love very strongly and very deeply. Men should always give women the utmost respect and love that they deserve.

If I could take back anything from my past when it came to women, I would take back the lying, disrespectful, and hateful way I behaved toward them. I can feel how much I've grown as a man over the years, and if I ever want to have that special lady in my life, I know I have to be considerate and respectful of their feelings, thoughts, and ambitions. I wish that no woman on earth should ever experience what I did to women. And if a man is behaving disrespectfully toward a woman, she must stand up for herself and make it known that such behavior is absolutely unacceptable.

I pray to God that one day I will find that special woman and finally be able to say those three important words: I love you.

"Let's increase the brand value of women."

~Melissa Dawn Johnson

A Gentleman's Cry

The Discussion

Chapter 12

The Discussion

What do men and women expect from each other?

Listen up, men. After sharing my story, which is full of difficult situations and environments, countless bad decisions, and a great deal of disrespect and abuse toward women, I started wondering what factors determine whether or not a relationship is successful and how we, as men, can achieve that kind of success. The first thing I knew was that whatever determines a happy relationship starts with our women. So I asked myself, "What is it that women want from men, for a man to be considered a great husband and, better yet, a great human being?" After talking to several women, I determined that most women want the following things:

1. Women want a man to be confident.
2. Women want a man who makes them feel like they are the only woman in the world.
3. Women want a man with a good sense of humor.
4. Women want a man who will listen to them.
5. Women want a man who will treat them like they are the sexiest woman he's ever seen.
6. Women want loyal men—they want to know you will be faithful.

7. Women want a man who is sensitive to their needs and the needs of others.

8. Women love a man with a plan; a man with ambition and goals.

9. Women want generous men. Don't be a tightwad; give the women in your life gifts every now and then to show her you are thinking of her.

10. Be a true friend. Most women want a man who is not only their lover, but also their best friend.

11. Women want to be loved despite their flaws, and need to be satisfied mentally, emotionally, and spiritually as much as they do physically.

12. Women appreciate a man who is creative. It shows that he challenges himself and is always thinking and looking for new ways to solve problems and experience life.

13. Women want a man who will offer her a sense of security. Women want to know that their partner will always be by their side, no matter what the situation.

So, to my men out there: if this is all that women want from us, why is it so hard for some of us to give them what they want and find that successful relationship? No one I asked, male or female, could answer this question with anything resembling a complete answer. Luckily, women can at least give us (mostly clueless) men an insight into the female mind. From them, I've learned that what women are looking for in a man can be generalized into four categories that explain the characteristics they find appealing.

1. **Confidence:**

   Most men either have no confidence or carry with them a false sense of confidence that they use to try to impress women. Women, just like men, want to see real confidence in a man's behavior and attitude, and they are sensitive to true confidence versus false bravado.

2. **Affection:**

   Showing affection is not solely a matter of physical contact or emotional connection, but a complex mix of the two. Women want to know that they are appreciated—everyone does—and this comes from affection and closeness as much as it does through any other aspect of a relationship.

3. **Security:**

   We live in an age where women can be truly independent. It is no longer true that a man must provide everything for his woman, but most women still like for their man to provide them with a sense of security. Now, security means more than simply bringing home the bacon or standing up for her honor. A woman wants to know that her partner is going to work at least as hard as she is to get the good things in life. Paying your bills and being financially honest with a woman are two great ways to prove that you are stable and can help ensure security in your relationship.

4. **Understanding:**

   Women are often stereotyped as overly emotional individuals; the truth is that all human beings are emotional, male and female alike. Being understanding means providing a shoulder to cry on, honest advice, and support during tough times. It is easy for us as men to overlook the little things that, when taken together, add up to being an understanding person. If your girlfriend is feeling moody, consider curling up under a blanket with her and watching her favorite television show together. Understanding is a vital component of a successful romantic relationship, and one that we men seem to struggle with the most.

Remember that every woman is different, and most women wouldn't appreciate their having desires generalized into the above four categories—I include them simply as food for thought for those men who may feel totally confused about women's desires. No human being is exactly the same as another, and you will no doubt find women who aren't looking for security or an understanding man. However, trying to be sensitive, confident, open to showing affection and stability, and trying to be emotionally open and understanding can only make you a better and more interesting man and, hopefully, a more appealing lover and partner.

Now that I have shared a little of what women may be looking for in a man, I'd like to address the ladies and talk about four things that men look for in a woman:

1. **Good Sex:**

   Let's not pretend that only men are looking for a capable and attentive sexual partner. Men want a partner who will be willing to share her affection physically without intimidating him. Besides, you can find out if you even like touching him long before committing to a date. Ladies, don't be intimidated by a man's desire for good sex—after all, isn't that something you want, too?

2. **Healthy Appearance:**

   Instead of trying to mold your body into someone else's idea of beauty, it's important to appreciate your own unique shape and work to maintain your health by taking care of yourself and practicing good hygiene. You have no say in whether or not a man is attracted to you, but you do have control over your health.

3. **Trust:**

   Here, trust refers not just to a man's ability to trust that his woman won't cheat on him, but to his ability to come to you for his emotional needs as well. If a man thinks you'll listen to his problems and then immediately run off to Twitter to your friends about it, he won't feel that sense of trust necessary to develop a healthy relationship. So how do you show a man that you are trustworthy? Avoid gossiping to him about your friends. It may seem fun, and yes, it's sometimes necessary to blow off steam, but it will teach him that you are an understanding person and that you take the problems of the people you care about seriously.

4. **Sense of Humor**

   Humor is a great icebreaker in many different situations. There will most certainly come a time in your relationship when a good joke will keep a minor disagreement from becoming a full-fledged argument. And laughter is also a great aphrodisiac. Men will find your sense of humor—no matter how goofy—a serious turn-on.

No two men are alike, and the desired traits in a girlfriend will differ from man to man. However, you can bet that some combination of the above features will attract just about any man.

A Gentleman's Cry

Blog: Questions and Answers

Chapter 13

Blog: Questions and Answers

I am currently single, so the chances of me being able to answer the questions I have posed are slim to none. My approach to this section was to ask these questions of both females and males and see what the differences in their answers and opinions would be. So let's blog!

Why is it that some women who are treated very poorly by their man continue to stay with him?

Female: Because we think we can change them.

Female: Some women allow it to happen; some women stay because of low self-esteem. A man will only go as far as you let him.

Male: Some people subject themselves to unnecessary pain and punishment. We have all faced trials and tribulations in relationships that tear at our heart and our soul.

Female: I let one treat me poorly over and over again because I loved him and I kept listening to his promises to change. Now I know that he is incapable of change and I wouldn't wish him on any sane woman.

If you have been seeing a man for awhile and you have not labeled your relationship as being "together" or "partners," what does it mean when a man tells you he is not ready? What is it he's not ready for?

Male: Not ready for commitment!

Male: When no lines have been established and someone says something like that, it means that things have already moved into that "together" stage, whether the man likes it or not!

Female: Sorry, he's just not that in to you. Move on. Staying with him is only keeping your true love from finding you!

Male: He could be feeling you a lot and see a real future with you, but he might not feel ready to give up the single life just yet.

Female: Regardless, a person who cuts off something that isn't even there is a waste of time.

Women: are you more attracted to a man for what he has and who is he rather than the man himself? What if he is broke with swagger—would you still be interested? Or what if he had no swagger and was kind of corny, but had lots of money?

Female: I'm attracted to a man I can trust. I trust men who are financially responsible. They don't have to be rich, by any means, only rich in love!

Men, are smart women intimidating?

Female: Smart women intimidate some men.

Male: Okay, a little, but it's kind of hot—very hot!

Female: Not sure many men will have the guts to answer this, but in some circumstances—yes.

How do women know what a real man is?

> **Male:** It's not about whether you're a good man or woman but about being a good human being. We get caught up in the nonsense. When you love yourself, you can easily love others around you.

Men, what do you look for in a woman? What are some characteristics you find appealing?

> **Male:** A strong, independent woman who can just be herself. Just keep it simple and sweet.

Why do men cheat? If they aren't happy why can't they just tell their mate so they can either work on it or move on?

> **Male:** Men cheat for all sorts of reasons. Sometimes it is simply because they can do it or because the opportunity is available, sometimes it is because the have low self-esteem, are unhappy at home, or are afraid of commitment and are just seeking fun.

Regarding friendship, is it possible for a guy to simply be friends with an attractive woman, or is he always waiting on an opportunity to get in (literally)?

> **Male:** With an underlying current of sexual attraction already there, the intimacy of a true friendship is at some point bound to cause a man to cross the line. And even if he doesn't cross the line, he will most certainly test the boundaries.

How long should a woman wait for a man to pop the question?

> **Male:** Anything more than one to two years is way too long. If he can't decide by then whether or not he loves, then tell him to hit the bricks. Many men are terrified of marriage and would prefer to live with their girlfriends, having all the benefits and

no responsibility, or just keep dating with no real commitment.

How long does it take for a man to introduce a woman to his family?

Male: There is no specific point in time that one must be introduced to their partner's family. The when is completely determined by the two people involved.

A Gentleman's Cry

Men, Know Your Place

Chapter 14

Men, Know Your Place

Within minutes of observing you or interacting with you, a woman will place you into one of three categories.

1. **Creep:**

   The creep is attracted to a woman but doesn't have the courage to openly interact with her, so he hovers around her, just hoping something will just happen. He's the guy who traces her mailing address and sends anonymous letters. He's the guy at the bar who will stare from a distance and when he's drunk enough, approach her without a smile and try to make stiff, serious conversation. Hint: Women run away from the creep.

2. **Provider (a.k.a., husband material):**

   The provider is the type of guy who treats attraction like a business deal. He buys the woman dinners and gifts and hopes she'll have a relationship with him in return. But that's not exactly how it works. When a man asks a woman, "Can I take you out to dinner," what she hears is, " I cannot have fun without you, so I'd like to buy you some food and make you see me as a provider. Then, hopefully, you'll accept me and make my life exciting." Hint:

Women usually don't have sex with the provider; they delay the sex until marriage.

3. **Lover:**

   The lover understands attraction. When he is interested in a woman and wants to spend time with her, he says, "I'm going to a wine-tasting workshop on Wednesday, would you like to come along?" What the woman hears is, " I'm already having a fun time without you. If you join me we can have fun together. But if you don't join me I'll still have fun." This is the kind of man that women desire sexually. Hint: Many women seek a provider type as a husband or boyfriend to pay the bills, while discreetly seeking a lover type on the side.

Even if you want a woman to see you as husband material, you have to first get her to see you as lover. It's easy to go from lover to husband, but not the other way around.

A Gentleman's Cry

Listen to Your Soul

Chapter 15

Listen to Your Soul

To all the men out there who are in search of that special someone or, better yet, have found that special relationship, I give you this to think about: When we become conflicted in relationships, it is often because our brain says one thing and our heart says another. We try to find a solution with our brains and react with our hearts. But the soul gets energy from both the mind and the heart; if we can learn to listen to our inner voice, our souls can be the arbitrator between the two. We must learn to listen, hear, and trust our soul's inner voice—it's never wrong.

If you have found a special lady but still aren't quite sure whether or not you are really in love with her, then read the list below and consider which of the statements apply to you.

- You are inspired to make her smile everyday.
- You give her a gift and it fills you with happiness.
- You look in her eyes and feel a jolt of positive energy.
- You are inspired to make her feel safe and loved.
- You desire and are filled with joy from her affection.

- You do just about anything you can to take care of her.
- You are inspired to be the best you can be for her.
- You are dedicated to the success of the relationship.
- You look at her and know that you are home.
- You look at her and your soul is at peace

If at least half of this list applies to you, then you have done the necessary things to better yourself and become a great man. You have found your special lady and that successful, happy relationship we are all seeking. I look forward to the day when I meet that special woman and am finally able check off all of the items on the list.

Women like acknowledgement and loving affection. They want a person with whom they can relate. They want a person they can trust. They want to be able to discuss problems they might be having, without difficulties. Women are mysterious, but they will show you what it feels like to be truly loved, as long as you're willing and able to accept the responsibility of a true loving relationship. You have to show them and mean it, no matter how hard it may be for you at the time. Women like men who are compassionate and understanding and someone who always genuinely cares. A woman wants a man to tell her often how important she is to him and show her that in his actions.

About the Author

Derrick Taylor, born and raised in Statesboro, Georgia now resides in Atlanta, Georgia. He opens up and gives you a glimpse into his soul by guiding you through his own personal journey. He's extremely enlightening and discusses challenges he's faced while giving a clear picture of what can be accomplished if you stay true to yourself and not lose sight in what you really want. In this book, *A Gentleman's Cry*, Derrick offers inspiration to those who want to take control of any crisis and become a better person. If he can do it, you can do it. Although change doesn't happens over night, Derrick is a man trying to figure out how to do better within his own personal life experiences and towards those surrounding him.

LaVergne, TN USA
07 April 2010
178408LV00005B/4/P

9 780615 360812